IMAGES
of America

MIAMI
The Magic City

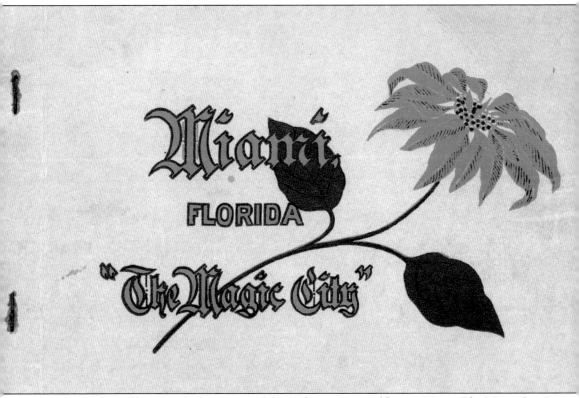

The Flagler publicists at the beginning of the 20th century would name Miami "the Magic City," and in this stunning 1925 color-photo booklet, that sobriquet was already in common usage, as shown on the cover.

ON THE COVER: It is the height of the great Florida "boom" of the 1920s, and we are looking east on Flagler Street from the corner of Miami Avenue in the midst of traffic, people, and business all meshing together at one of the greatest moments in Miami history. The trolley cars are packed, the police officers on the corner can't lose their concentration for a moment, and everybody is in a rush to buy land and property and turn it for a profit. The bust that would begin with the sinking of the four-masted schooner *Prinz Valdemar* in early 1926 and would be the harbinger of the Great Depression that would begin in the rest of the country in 1929 was not even in people's imaginations.

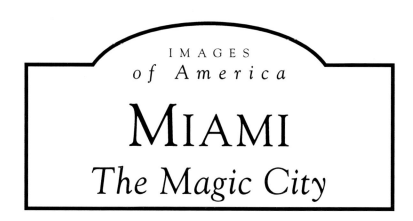

IMAGES
of America

MIAMI
The Magic City

Seth H. Bramson

ARCADIA
PUBLISHING

Published by Arcadia Publishing
Charleston, South Carolina

Printed in the United States of America

Library of Congress Catalog Card Number: 2006932623

For all general information contact Arcadia Publishing at:
Telephone 843-853-2070
Fax 843-853-0044
E-mail sales@arcadiapublishing.com
For customer service and orders:
Toll-Free 1-888-313-2665

Visit us on the Internet at www.arcadiapublishing.com

Dedicated to Miami's early pioneers. Many were their hardships and privations. Great was their courage, vision, and faith in the future.

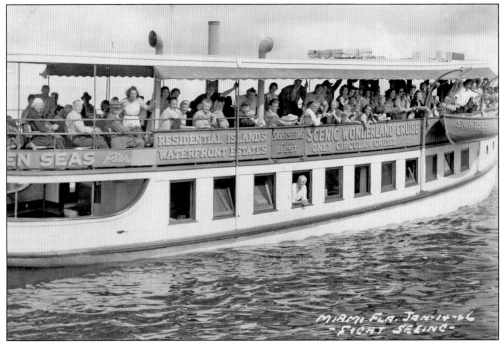

Miami and water are synonymous, and the tie-in has been almost as much a part of the city's history as its relationship with the Florida East Coast Railway. In this January 14, 1946, view, taken just a few months after World War II ended, the sightseeing boat *Seven Seas* takes a group of happy tourists (and, perhaps, some residents) on the famous "Scenic Wonderland Cruise."

CONTENTS

Acknowledgments   6

Introduction   7

1.   The Pioneers   9

2.   Henry Flagler, the FEC Railway,
     and the Royal Palm Hotel   29

3.   The Time of the Trolley   43

4.   A City Booms—and Then Busts   55

5.   Struggling through the Depression   87

6.   World War II and Its Aftermath   101

7.   A World-Class City Moves toward the Future   119

ACKNOWLEDGMENTS

In preparing a book about this fabled and incredible city, a diligent and thoughtful writer should take extra care in selecting photographs and images that have not been used numerous times before in other books and articles; hence, the bulk of the views herein are from the author's collection of Miami memorabilia. However, there are several people who deserve to be warmly acknowledged for their timely assistance in loaning rare photographs or memorabilia or who offered highly constructive thoughts and ideas as I moved forward with this project. First, of course, my wife of 30-plus years, my dear and beloved Myrna, once again patiently listened to my readings of various chapter introductions and captions and did not hesitate to offer suggestions for the better. Her love and unending patience are evident in the fact that, through it all, she remains at my side (to quote the late, great Rodney Dangerfield, "it's tough being me," but it's even tougher putting up with me). Kathleen Gillette, Jay Sweeney, and Norma Orovitz of the Miami Jewish Home and Hospital at Douglas Gardens so very graciously provided two marvelous photographs of the home; Gail and Mario Talucci, our longtime friends, searched their collection and found several stunning items, including the great view of the interior of the Olympia Theater shown on page 86; Mary Berke and her daughters, Barbara Poliacoff and Susan Frank, kindly loaned me Harold Berke's 1932 Miami High graduation exercises booklet; and Dr. Susannah Worth, curator of the Barnacle Historic State Park, was never too busy to answer my numerous questions. I am, indeed, so very appreciative of the thoughts and suggestions offered by friends and others interested in the history of this great city.

EAT AT THE WONDER BAR CAFE

23 N. E. FIRST AVENUE—SHORELAND ARCADE

EXCELLENT FOOD

Beef Stew with Fresh Vegetables 20c
Roast Leg of Lamb with Mashed Potatoes 29c
Saulsbury Steak with Mashed Potatoes 20c
Hot Roast Beef Sandwich, Mashed Potatoes 20c
Broiled King Fish with Mashed Potatoes 20c
Bread and Butter served with above orders

SPECIAL

Broiled T-Bone Steak, French Fried Potatoes, Salad 35c
2 Broiled Lamb Chops, French Fried Potatoes, Salad 35c
Minute Steak. French Fried Potatoes, Salad 25c
Fried Filet of Sole, French Fried Potatoes, Salad 25c
Hot Rolls and Butter served with above orders

Sandwiches with Salad, 10c and 15c

Soups, 5c and 10c   All Pies 5c and 10c cut
Pudding or Cobbler, 5c   Coffee or Tea, 5c

POPULAR PRICES

The Wonder Bar Café in the Shoreland Arcade (named for the company that was building Miami Shores) was just off of Flagler Street on Northeast First Avenue and was a terrific place during the 1920s and early 1930s to grab a quick bite or a cold drink. Lamb chops were 35¢.

INTRODUCTION

The question "Is another Miami book necessary" is valid only to those who feel that they have a patent on proffering Miami's history. The fact is that the last Miami history was done more than 10 years ago, in 1996, during the city's centennial year, and this book is the first and only detailed photographic history, using primarily images from the author's collection, of what is now one of the world's greatest, best-known, and most exciting cities. Further, this is the first and only photographic history that focuses and concentrates solely on the city of Miami and does not extend into other areas of Miami-Dade County.

The story of Julia Tuttle, William and Mary Brickell, the Sewell brothers, Commodore Ralph Munroe, the Peacocks, Isadore Cohen, the Burdines, D. A. Dorsey, the Stirrups of Coconut Grove, Dr. James A. Jackson, and so many other pioneers is well known and has been told no few times, but the presentation of that story in a unique photographic format such as this is a first.

Miami's springing into existence as a city on July 28, 1896, without ever having been a village, town, or other incorporated area is well documented, but in order to give a true and factual picture of how it happened, the "Orange Blossom Myth" must first be debunked.

The story that Julia Tuttle, the "Mother of Miami," sent Henry Flagler, the builder of Florida's east coast, some orange blossoms and that he then extended the railroad to what would become Miami is pure hype. Tuttle had, for several years, been beseeching first Henry Plant (famous for his building of railroads and hotels in Central Florida and on the state's west coast) and then Henry Flagler to connect the settlement on the shores of Biscayne Bay to the rest of the state by rail, but neither felt that doing so would be economically viable.

Plant, tiring of Tuttle's frequent missives, abruptly told her that he did not wish to hear further from her and that he had no intention of extending his railroad 160 miles across the Everglades to satisfy her ego. Flagler, who had known her father in Cleveland, was equally firm but much less final, simply thanking her for writing and explaining the reasons for his declination.

In December 1894 and January and February 1895, the worst freezes ever to hit the Florida peninsula destroyed the citrus crop all the way south into the center of Dade County, which at that time extended from Indian Key in the middle of the Florida Keys (all now Monroe County) to north of Jupiter in what is now Palm Beach County.

The region south of the New River below Fort Lauderdale, and particularly in the area closer to the Tuttle and Brickell homesteads, was untouched by the freezes. Tuttle wasted no time in contacting Flagler, and he, in turn, dispatched his now-famous lieutenants James E. Ingraham (for whom Miami's Ingraham Building is named), the Flagler System's land commissioner, and Joseph R. Parrott, Flagler's railroad vice-president, to furthest South Florida to verify Tuttle's claim and to report back to him. He was nothing if not skeptical.

Ingraham and Parrott returned to Palm Beach laden with citrus, produce, and whole boughs and limbs of fruit trees wrapped in wet cotton. Flagler was amazed, and he wired Tuttle, "Madam, what is it that you propose?"

Tuttle replied that if Flagler would extend his railroad to the shores of Biscayne Bay and build one of his magnificent hotels, she would give him half of her holdings north of the river plus 50 acres for railroad shops and yards, and Mr. Brickell would give Flagler half of his holdings south of the river. A deal was struck, a contract was signed, and the building of the railroad south of Palm Beach began.

Construction began almost simultaneously on the Royal Palm Hotel under the direction of Flagler's man in Miami, John Sewell. On April 15, 1896, the first train, a materials and equipment train, reached the settlement. One week later, the first passenger train arrived. On May 15, 1896, the first edition of the *Miami Metropolis* (later to become the *Miami Daily News*) was published, and on July 28, 1896, either 343 or 344 (as with today's Miami, the number of votes in any election varies, depending on who is counting) of the 502 eligible adults, including no few black people, voted to incorporate Miami as a city. On December 31, 1896, the Royal Palm opened with a gala New Year's Eve ball. Sadly Julia Tuttle would die of influenza in 1898, never getting to see the city she was responsible for founding grow into the great metropolis she knew it would become.

In 1895, Isadore Cohen, the first permanent Jewish settler, arrived and within just a few years, people such as Burdine, Sewell, Budge, the great black property owner and merchant D. A. Dorsey, Merrick (father and son), Frow, Peacock, Munroe, Douthit, Gaskins, Hy Hyman of Florida Power and Light, and others would begin the task—which continues even today—of building and rebuilding a city.

The story of Miami is one of the most incredible stories of city-building in American history. From World War I through the boom, bust, Depression, World War II, the 1950s, the great Cuban immigration of the 1960s through 1990s, and the growth that some think is overwhelming, the Miami story never gets old; it simply becomes more and more fascinating and mesmerizing with every change of the season and every turn of the pages of history.

One

THE PIONEERS

The history of what would eventually become Miami actually goes back to the Paleo-Indian era. Former Dade County archaeologist Robert Carr has determined, by the finding of the fossils, that the Miami area was a savanna and that among the fauna were mastodons, saber-tooth tigers, giant sloths, and other now-extinct animals. Along with them, there were people.

It is difficult to determine how far south the Timucuans and Calusas came. The fierce Arawaks of the Caribbean might have spent some time in the area, but the first identifiable artifacts are those of the Tequestas, a tribe that faded from sight as the Miccosukees and Seminoles gained strength and population. The Tequestas are commemorated by having the yearly scholarly journal of the Historical Association of Southern Florida named for them.

Eventually, through three wars, the Seminoles were pushed deeper and deeper into the Everglades, and Bahamians eventually settled what became Coconut Grove. Ralph Munroe first visited South Florida in 1877, and in 1882, he helped open the Bay View Villa (later the Peacock Inn), the area's first hostelry.

Munroe, known as the Commodore, served for 22 years as the leader of the Biscayne Bay Yacht Club and built a home that is today a cherished Miami landmark. Known as the Barnacle, the home is the centerpiece of the state park in Coconut Grove.

John Sewell came to the area on behalf of Henry Flagler and supervised the building of the Royal Palm, later inducing his brother, Everest ("Ev"), to join him, the latter becoming a popular politician and mayor in the 1920s and 1930s.

While the Sewell brothers claimed to operate "Miami's first store," Roddy Burdine expanded his family's emporium, Burdine's. It would later become one of America's great retail names, much beloved by Miamians, until being subsumed by Federated Department Stores' Macy's chain.

Other individuals and families added to the potpourri, whether of Bahamian origin, American blacks, or whites from the Midwest or Northeast. The appeal of the sparkling jewel on the banks of the Miami River eventually extended into the American psyche and, like a magnet, began to draw attention—and people—to the growing city on the shores of Biscayne Bay.

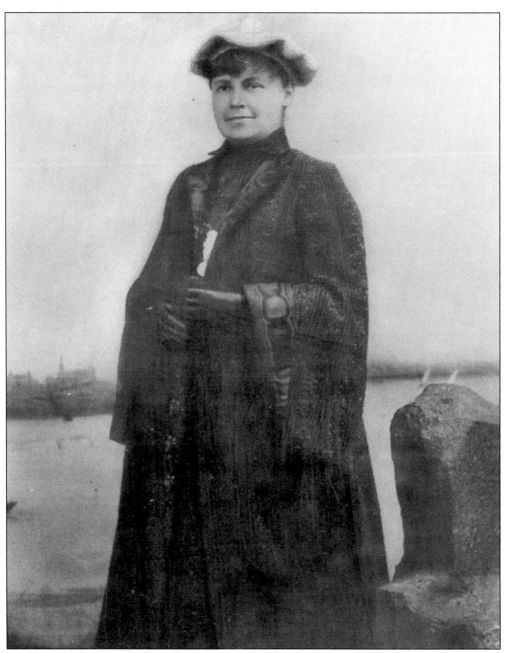

Julia DeForest Sturtevant Tuttle (January 22, 1849–September 14, 1898) came to the banks of the Miami River with her household goods and her two children, Fannie and Harry, in 1891. Clearing the vines and tangles of weeds surrounding the old Fort Dallas buildings that she had purchased, she looked at the wilderness along the Miami River and saw not mangroves and coconut palms but a thriving city. Sadly she would never get to see the city she envisioned come into existence.

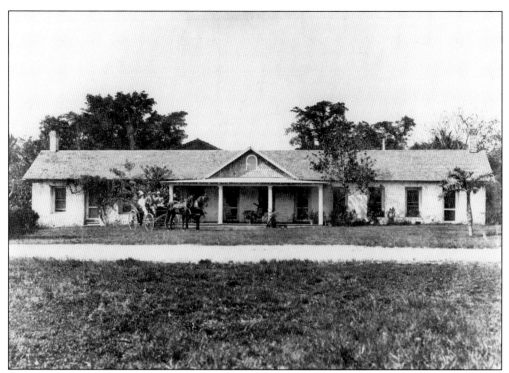

A view of the old Fort Dallas barracks shows the property that became the Tuttle homestead. Although undated, it is believed that this photograph shows Julia Tuttle in the carriage on the left side of the image.

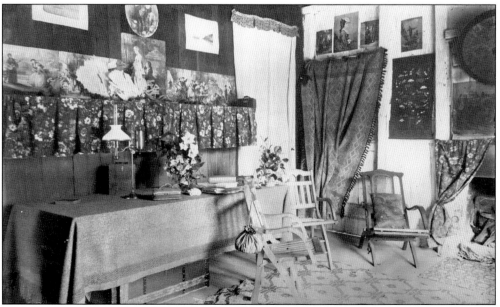

One of the rarest Miami photographs known to exist shows one of the rooms—likely a sitting room—in the house of te Three Sisters in Coconut Grove. The photograph on the far right on the wall to the right may be the sharpie "Kingfisher." Original photograph by Ralph Munroe, collection of Historical Museum of Southern Florida.

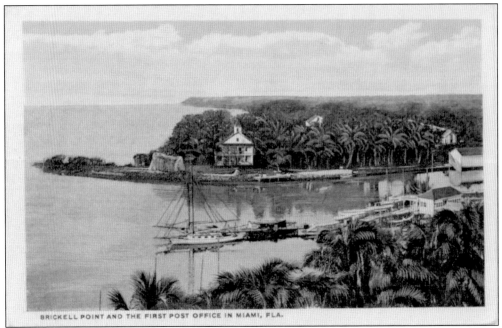

BRICKELL POINT AND THE FIRST POST OFFICE IN MIAMI, FLA.

The caption on this very early Miami postcard identifies Brickell Point and the first post office. The Brickell trading post is prominent on the south bank of the Miami River. Further south, in the distance, is the village of Cocoanut Grove (the "a" was later removed from the name). On the close right (north bank) are the boathouses of the Royal Palm Hotel.

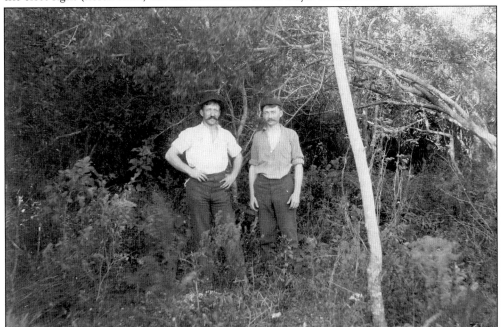

Miami pioneers Charles Mohl (left) and Henry Kaiser pose somewhere in the Miami hammock, likely near the river. Both would become founders of the Miami Pioneers, now merged with the Natives of Dade. Many members of the organization are also members of the Miami Memorabilia Collectors Club.

It is not possible to make out Captain Killum's first name on this photograph, but his early claim to fame in Miami's history is that he married one of the Brickell girls. This Richard Chamberlain photograph, taken in Chamberlain's Miami studio at the beginning of the 20th century, is important as much for showing Killum as for having Chamberlain's name and "Miami" at the bottom of the photograph jacket.

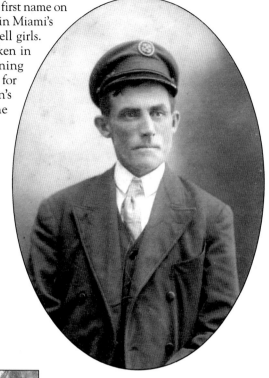

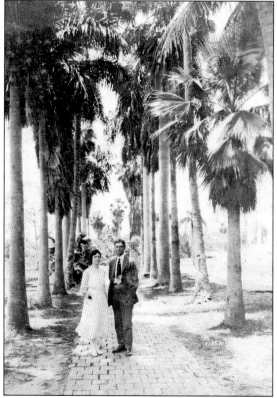

Harry Budge opened Miami's first hardware store, and for years, it was located on the northeast corner of Twelfth Street and Avenue D, later renamed Flagler Street and Miami Avenue. The Budge Hardware Company lasted into the 1970s, and several of Harry's descendants are still proud Miamians. Here a young Harry and his lovely bride, Gussie, are on the palm walk of the Royal Palm Hotel.

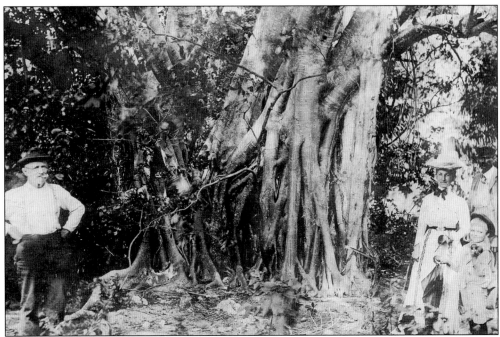

This incredible banyan tree, already a senior citizen when this photograph was taken around 1900, stood in the citrus grove of another Miami pioneer, Samuel Filer. The grove was located at what is now Northeast Twenty-sixth Street east of today's Biscayne Boulevard, adjacent to Biscayne Bay.

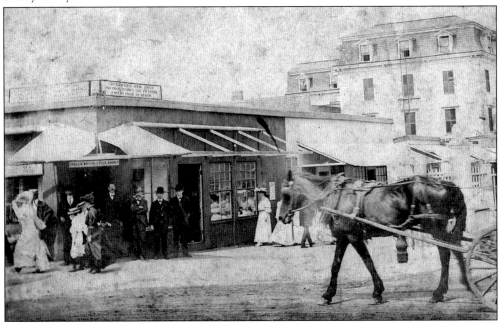

This never-before-published view shows Sulzner's Gem Shop, identified by Miami Memorabilia Collectors Club member and genealogist Larry Wiggins as one of the city's earliest jewelry stores, possibly the first. Sulzner's also served for several years as the Indian Motorcycle Agency for the city, and the sign proclaiming that fact hangs from beneath the awning at left center.

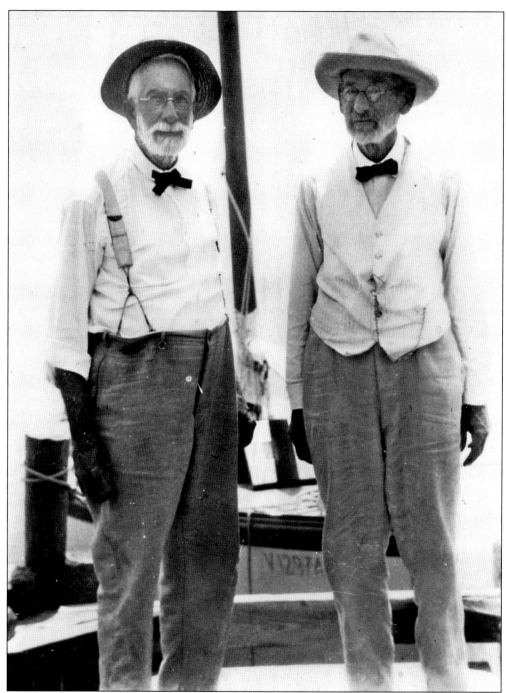

In this photograph, Miami and Coconut Grove Pioneer Commodore Ralph Middleton Munroe stands at left, naval architect Nat Hereshoff at right. According to Dr. Susannah Worth, curator of the Barnacle Historic State Park in Coconut Grove, the Commodore arrived several years before Julia Tuttle and, along with several others, founded the Biscayne Bay Yacht Club in 1887, serving as commodore for 22 years. (Ralph Munroe photogrpah, Historical Museum of Southern Florida).

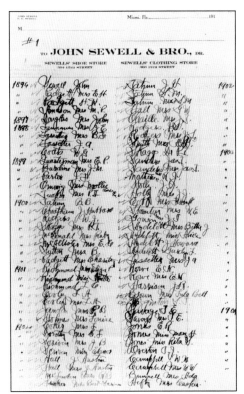

John and Ev Sewell claimed to have opened Miami's first store, and that legend appears on promotional items the brothers issued, including shoe brushes. This letterhead contains the names of several Miami pioneers, and while the author is unsure of the reason that it was written, it is, at the least, a genealogical treasure.

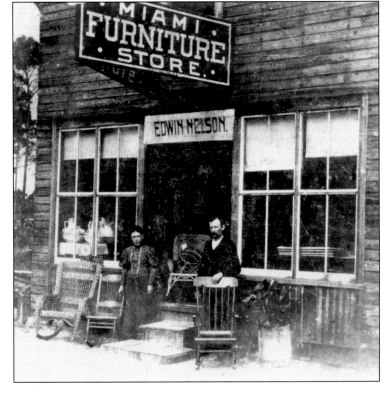

The Miami Furniture Store, owned by Edwin Nelson, was located in one of the wooden buildings on Twelfth Street (later Flagler Street) that burned in the November 1899 fire, which destroyed much of what was then downtown. The fire would be the catalyst for one of the earliest rebuildings of the city.

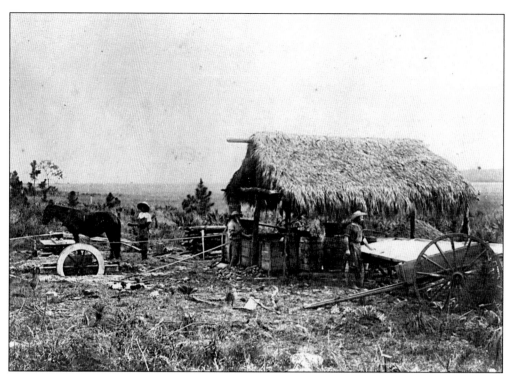

In the late years of the 19th and early years of the 20th centuries, the Everglades were a forbidding place, but as civilization crept steadily westward, agriculture began to expand, and the Everglades receded. In this pre-1907 view, the difficulties of farming in what had been Everglades (now just west of Northwest Twelfth Avenue) are quite evident.

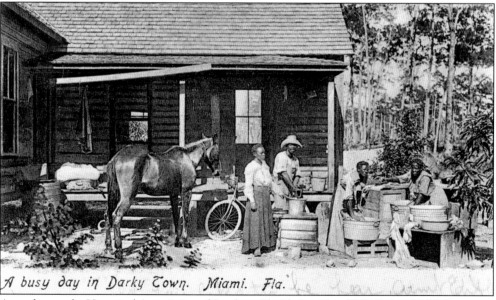

A busy day in Darky Town. Miami. Fla.

According to the Historical Association of Southern Florida President/CEO Robert H. McCammon, this view is Charles Peacock's coontie mill, at present day MacFarlane Road and Main Highway in Coconut Grove. (Ralph Munroe photogrpah, Historical Museum of Southern Florida).

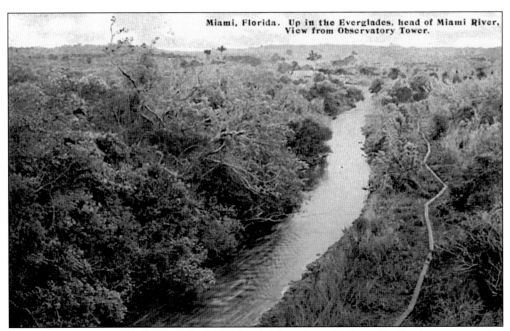

Miami, Florida. Up in the Everglades, head of Miami River. View from Observatory Tower.

From earliest times until the arrival of the Florida East Coast Railway (FEC), the river was the lifeblood and main artery of transportation for the few settlers and the natives who inhabited the region. The water was fresh and safe to drink; children swam and played in it; and the fish and crabs caught in it were safe to eat. Sadly that all changed with the laying of the sewer pipe from the Royal Palm Hotel directly into the river, and with the dredging and destruction of the pristine environment, the Miami River would be unrecognizable within a relatively few years. Lower photograph taken in Coconut Grove by Ralph Munroe, courtesy of Marilyn Catlow, original negative in collection of Historical Museum of Southern Florida.

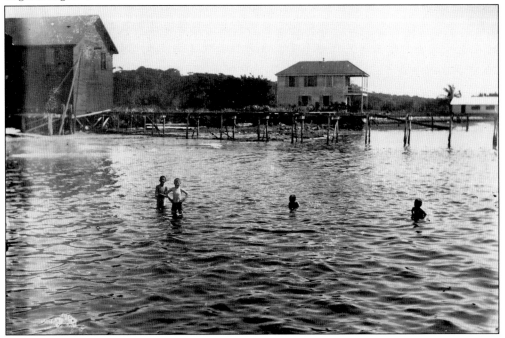

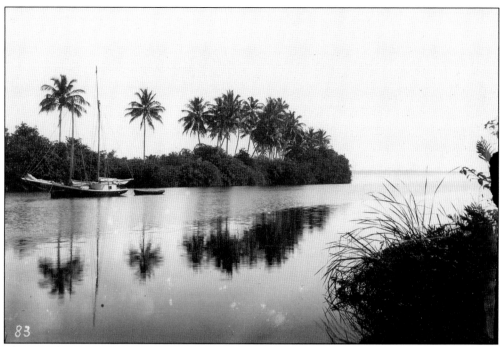

The view looks east toward Biscayne Bay from the south bank of the river at or close to the time of the arrival of the Brickells and Tuttle and her children. As can be seen, the vista was of a pristine beauty nearly beyond description.

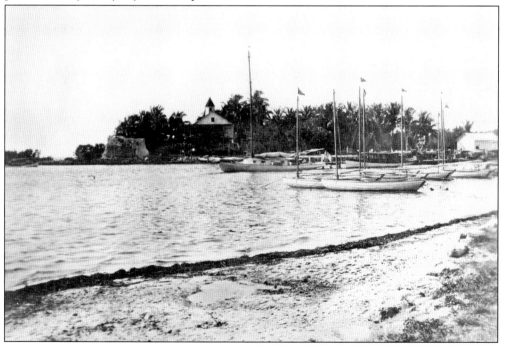

A view rarely if ever before seen, and likely never before published, this photograph was taken on the north bank of the river looking south toward the Brickell home and trading post. The only thing that remains from that period is the water; nothing else is recognizable.

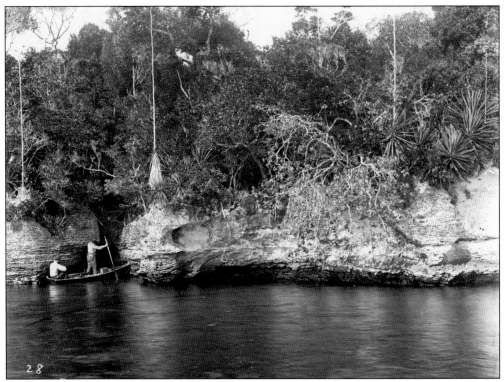

The waters of Biscayne Bay were as inviting and beautiful as the early Miami River, and cruising slowly south from the river there were innumerable places to explore, picnic, or relax. The two boaters have pulled their skiff into an indentation in the limestone, likely to look it over, while the man squatting in front of the Devil's Punch Bowl in the pre-1909 view appears delighted to have found this still-existing but well-hidden natural anomaly.

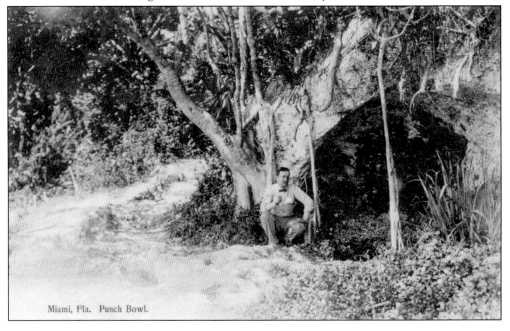

Miami, Fla. Punch Bowl.

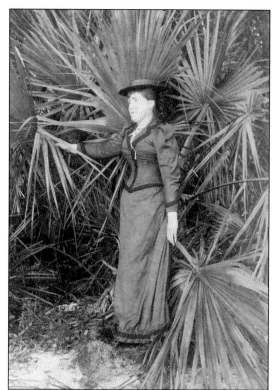

While there is no indication of who the woman is in this very early Miami photograph taken in the midst of cabbage palm fronds, the young fellow on the bicycle is J. K. Dorn. The picture of Dorn was taken in 1898 by Otto Erasmus of the Hand Studio, shown on page 28. Before the automobile, bicycles were a favored means of local transportation in the blooming city.

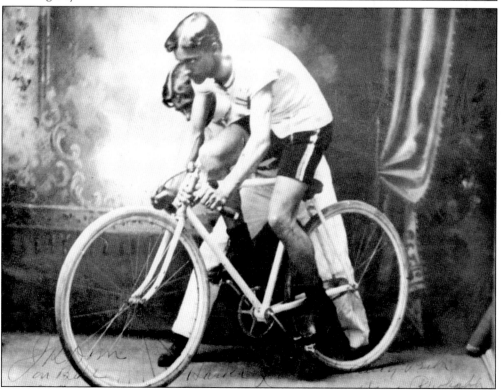

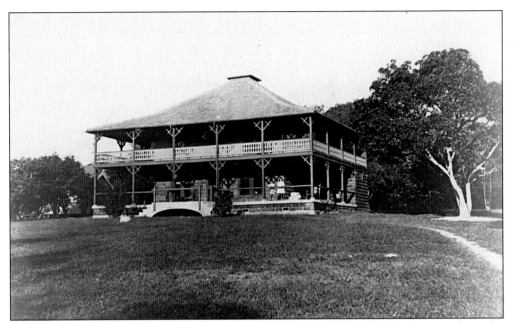

According to Dr. Susannah Worth the Barnacle was originally built as a one story home by Commodore Munroe in 1891. In 1908, the home was enlarged and made into a two story house as shown here. It is believed that the Barnacle is the oldest house in it's original location in Miami-Dade County today. (Photograph courtesy of Mailyn Catlow).

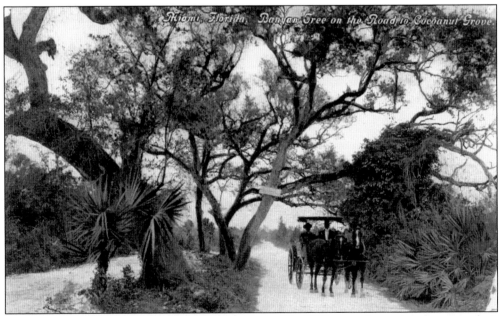

Getting to Coconut Grove in pioneer days was a trip. The FEC opened a station there at today's Douglas Road, just west of South Dixie Highway, but it was a lengthy hike into the main business and residential areas. Many people used horses or horse-drawn transportation such as this carriage passing the banyan tree on the road to Coconut Grove, most likely today's South Bayshore Drive.

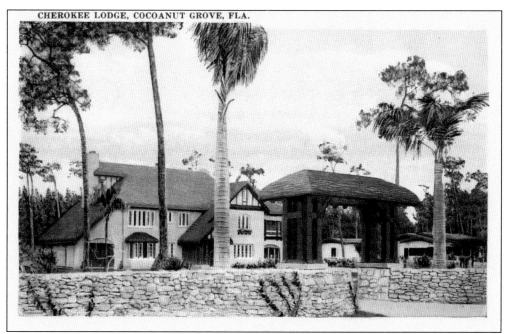

The Cherokee Lodge in Cocoanut Grove (the original spelling included an "a" that is no longer used) was a monumental structure for its time. Still in existence, it is a private home across from the Carrollton School.

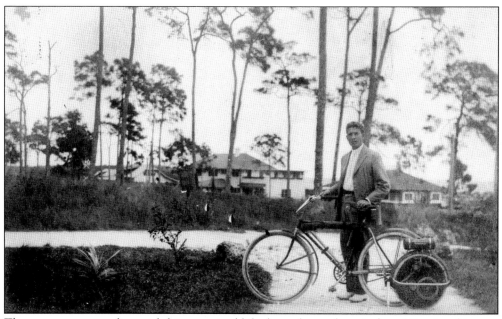

The young man standing with his motorized bike has taken a day trip from Miami and is seen in front of another of the beautiful early Coconut Grove buildings.

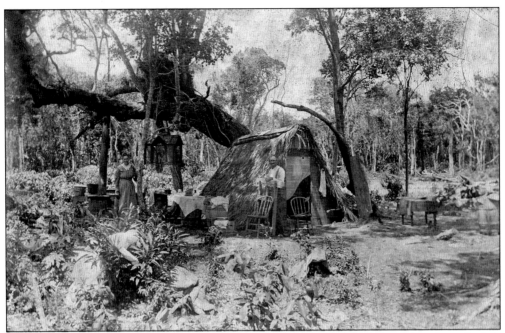

In early Miami, homes ran the gamut from the most rudimentary to having shingle roofs. It is quite a contrast to see the palm-thatch-roofed house, complete with table and chairs outside for al fresco dining (although likely not thought of that way at the time) along with the first shingle-roofed house in the area (below), belonging to Mr. and Mrs. L. E. Hill and their nephew, Joe Byrd, shown in front of their house. This incredible Miami photograph was taken in 1896 by an unknown photographer.

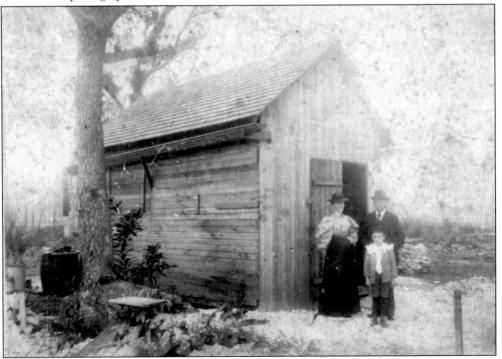

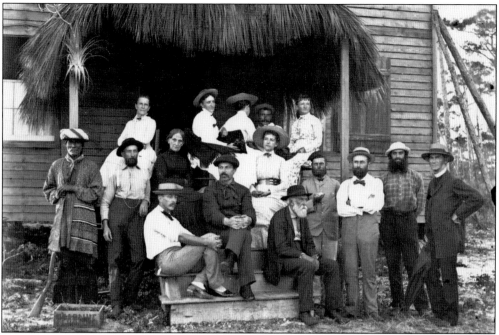

This wonderful photograph of early Miamians was taken by Ralph Munroe during the season of 1886–1887 in Coconut Gove, which was the first winter resort on Biscayne Bay and show, in the top row, left to right, Mrs. Thomas Munroe, Flora McFarlane, Mrs. Kirk Munroe, Edward A. Hine, and Mrs. Thomas A. Hine; middle row Doctor Tiger, R. M. Munroe, and Mrs. E. P. Brown; seated Kirk Munroe, Count Jean d'Hedouville, and Alfred Munroe. (Photo from Marilyn Catlow, original negative now in collection of Historical Museum of Southern Florida).

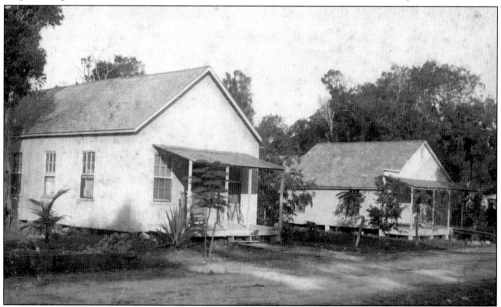

Quite substantial for the time, these two houses were either in what was then North Miami (between Seventh and First Streets) or in Southside, which later would become the Roads area, so named because the street suffix in the area is "Road."

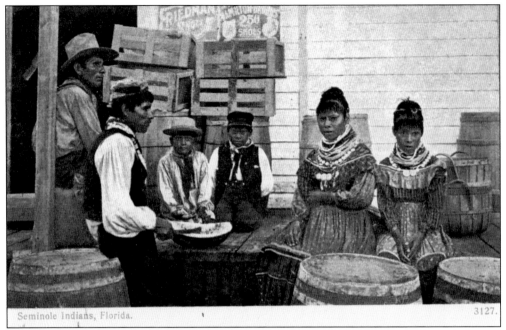

Seminole Indians, Florida.   3127.

While not overlooked, the Seminole tribe has not received its appropriate due in the early history of Miami. Whether as trappers, fishermen, or merchants, they played a great part in the growth of the city. Here a group of Seminoles sits outside one of Miami's early stores.

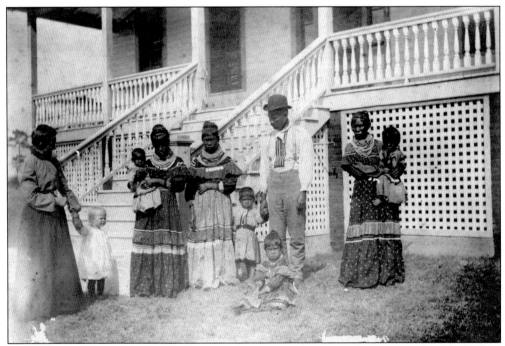

It is an exciting moment when pioneers are identified in the very early photographs. On the left, Mrs. Charles Mann, with her daughter, visits with a Seminole family group in front of one of the pioneer homes.

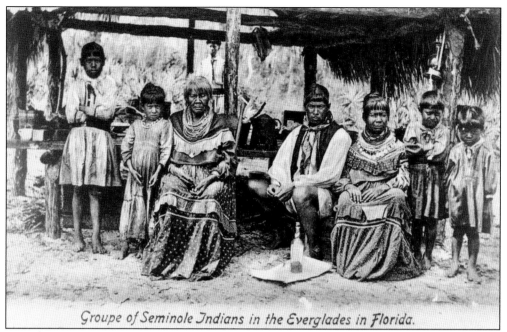

Groupe of Seminole Indians in the Everglades in Florida.

Another group of Seminoles is shown sitting in front of the chickee that was their home. Chickees (Seminole for *house*) could be easily disassembled and moved if needed, most likely a trait that was a holdover from the three Seminole wars, when it was necessary for them to be able to move quickly to elude U.S. cavalry.

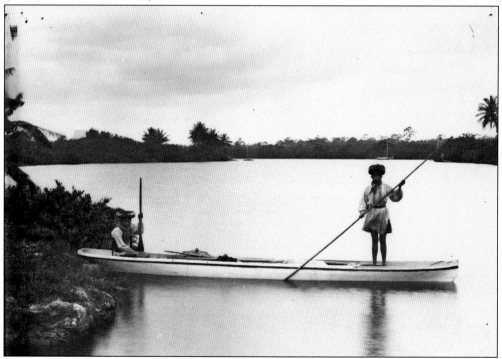

Standing in a dugout canoe, one Native American is the poler while the other keeps rifle at the ready should he see game on the banks as they move silently up or down the Miami River.

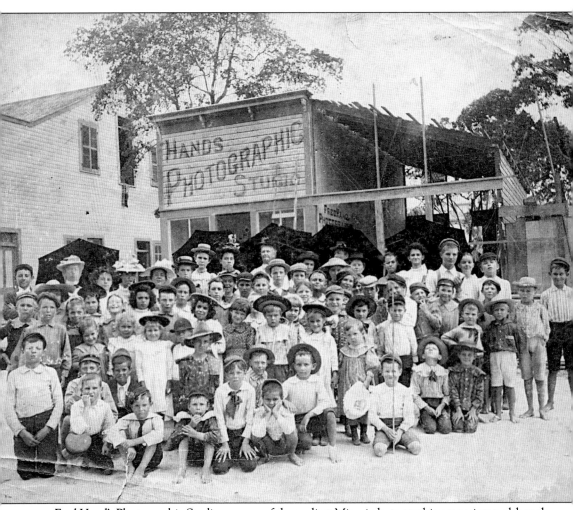

Fred Hand's Photographic Studio was one of the earliest Miami photographic emporiums, although the Hand name rarely surfaces; apparently the firm either folded or Hand left Miami quite early. However, this magnificent photograph of a school group shows not only the children and their teachers but also the studio on Twelfth (now East Flagler) Street around 1905.

Two

HENRY FLAGLER, THE FEC RAILWAY, AND THE ROYAL PALM HOTEL

Henry Morrison Flagler is the single greatest and most revered name in the history of Florida. His deeds, achievements, and accomplishments are legendary, and yet his importance to Miami has never received its full due. Simply put, were there no Flagler, Miami would be completely different than it is today, and its July 28, 1896, birth would assuredly have been delayed for years. While the east coast of Florida is his monument, Miami needs to do more to memorialize Henry Flagler.

In September 1895, the name of the Jacksonville, St. Augustine, and Indian River Railway was changed to Florida East Coast Railway, and to railroad buffs and American historians, that name is both uttered and written with reverence, for the FEC is one of the few railroads that has not been gobbled up by the giants. Its history is of such interest and importance that it merits its own society of loyal and faithful fans, supported and encouraged by a management that is as astute and insightful as it is forward looking and progressive.

The official date for the arrival of the railroad in Miami—the date furnished to the Interstate Commerce Commission by the railroad—is April 15, 1896. In July 1996, the railroad and the city celebrated their 100th anniversary together in a gala weekend culminating on Sunday, July 28, 1996, complete with an FEC train on display in downtown Miami.

The Flagler-owned FEC Hotel Company built the Royal Palm Hotel. Opening with a gala ball on December 31, 1896, it would become the center of Miami's social and business activities until it was severely damaged in the 1926 hurricane. Opening briefly during the 1928 season, it closed abruptly, never to reopen. In 1930, the fabulous hotel was torn down board by board, the contents and fixtures sold to Miami residents. With the loss of the hotel and the onset of the Depression, a great and glorious period in Miami history came to an end.

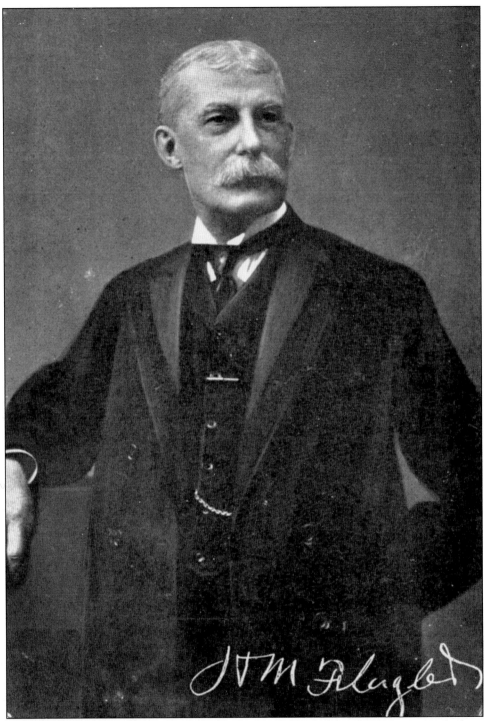

He is unquestionably our founder, and no other name in Miami or Florida history carries the legacy and imprimatur of Henry M. Flagler. Born January 2, 1830, in Hopewell, New York, his death on May 20, 1913, was memorialized by almost every newspaper in America, and his greatness and glory will remain intact as long as there is a Florida.

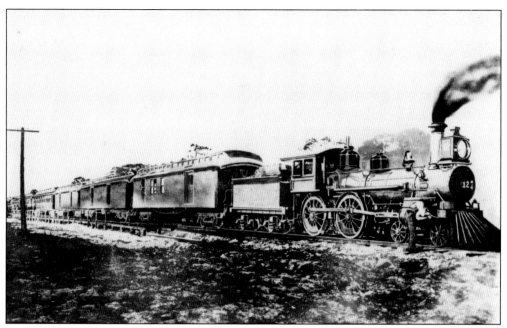

It is related to FEC and Miami historians that steam locomotive No. 12, with a seven-car passenger train including a U.S. Railway Mail Service post office car directly behind the locomotive, was the first engine into Miami. This photograph, much retouched, is the famous image, complete with smoke blowing the wrong way!

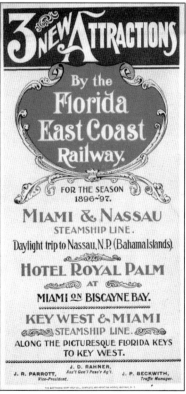

To coincide with the opening of the Royal Palm Hotel in time for the 1897 season, the Flagler companies issued this heavy-stock fold-over announcing trips to Nassau and Key West along with the opening of the hotel. Much sought after by Florida collectors, this is one of the very few known to exist.

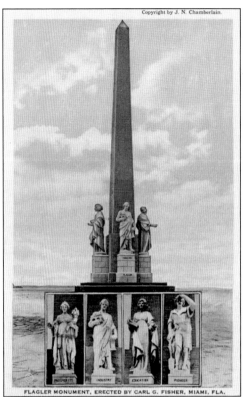

FLAGLER MONUMENT, ERECTED BY CARL G. FISHER, MIAMI, FLA.

Carl Fisher, builder of Miami Beach, would create the single greatest and most impressive monument dedicated to the founder, and this statue on Monument Island is maintained by the city. Below each statue is a title memorializing all that Flagler did for Miami and the state: Prosperity, Industry, Education, and Pioneer.

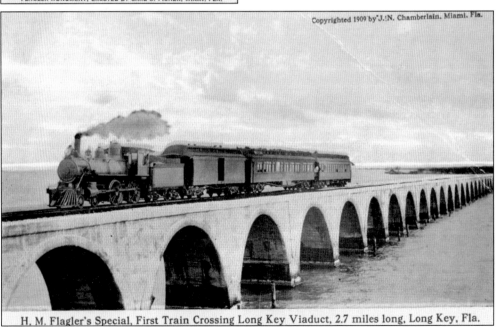

H. M. Flagler's Special, First Train Crossing Long Key Viaduct, 2.7 miles long, Long Key, Fla.

With all that Flagler did in and for Florida, his most monumental work was the building of the Key West Extension, the greatest railway engineering and construction feat in American (and possibly world) history. His special train is shown crossing Long Key Viaduct, the first train to make the trip over that beautiful bridge.

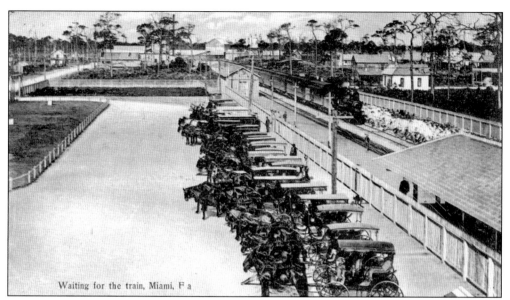

Waiting for the train, Miami, F a

The first Miami passenger station was essentially a shed located at Twelfth (Flagler) Street and the tracks. As quickly as possible, the FEC erected a beautiful station between today's Northeast Second Avenue and Biscayne Boulevard on the site where the Miami News Building would be built. The station remained there from late 1896 until the new station opened at Avenue E and Tenth Street (later 200 Northwest First Avenue) in late 1912 as part of the Key West Extension improvements.

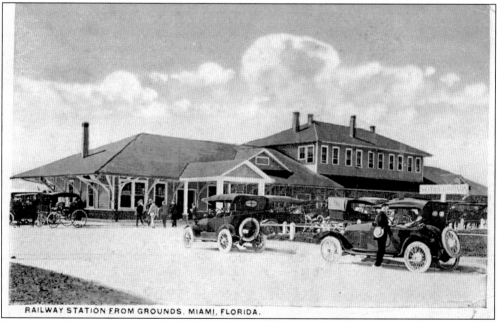

RAILWAY STATION FROM GROUNDS, MIAMI, FLORIDA.

From late 1912 until the end of passenger service on January 22, 1963, the venerable depot at 200 Northwest First Avenue would handle FEC's passenger train services—sometimes, at the height of the great Florida boom, as many as 50 to 60 movements per day. Beginning in September 1963, as a result of the strike by non-operating unions, the station was dismantled and a great era of Miami's history came to a distressing and ignominious end.

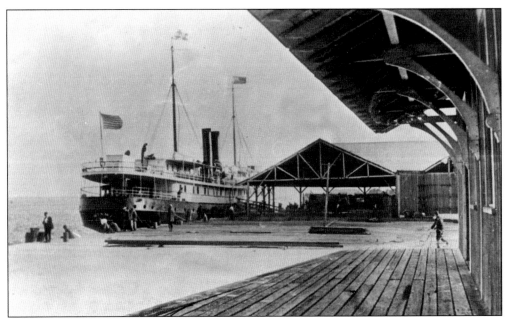

In conjunction with the opening of the Miami depot on (old) Sixth Street, the FEC extended its tracks across the narrow street then known as the Boulevard to the Flagler-owned Peninsular and Occidental Steamship Company (P&O) docks and built a second station for the comfort of the connecting steamship passengers. Here the SS *Miami* is waiting to depart for Nassau in the Bahamas around 1904.

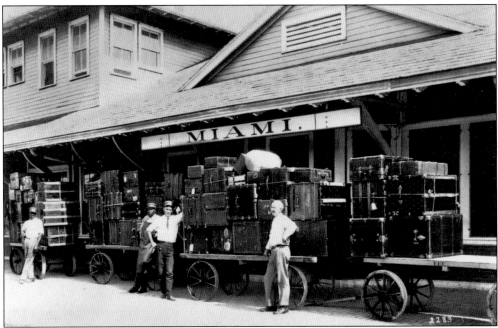

Even after the new station opened, service was still provided to the P&O docks. However, the necessity for the new station is shown in this never-before-published view featuring the stationmaster on the right and porters waiting to begin loading the immense quantities of baggage and express pouring into and out of the city.

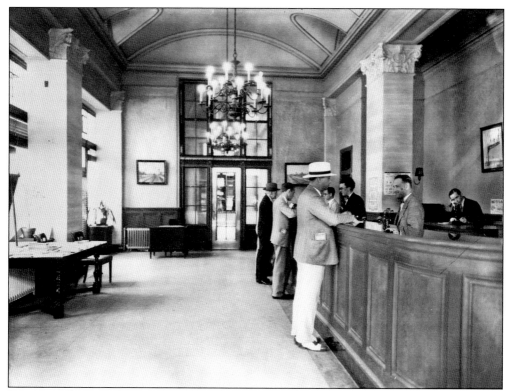

Passengers thronged the FEC Miami City Ticket Office after it opened in the Ingraham Building at the corner of Southeast Second Avenue and First Street. The ticket clerk in the center is the late William Wooten, who would become the railway's ticket agent at the passenger station and was promoted to stationmaster before retiring with the onset of the 1963 strike. The door directly in front of the camera leads to the Ingraham Building lobby.

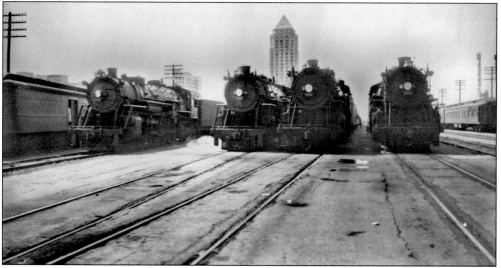

Four of FEC's 400-series fast passenger engines await the highball to carry business people and vacationers north. On some days during the boom and World War II, arriving trains had to wait for departures until tracks were clear in order for them to enter the station to unload.

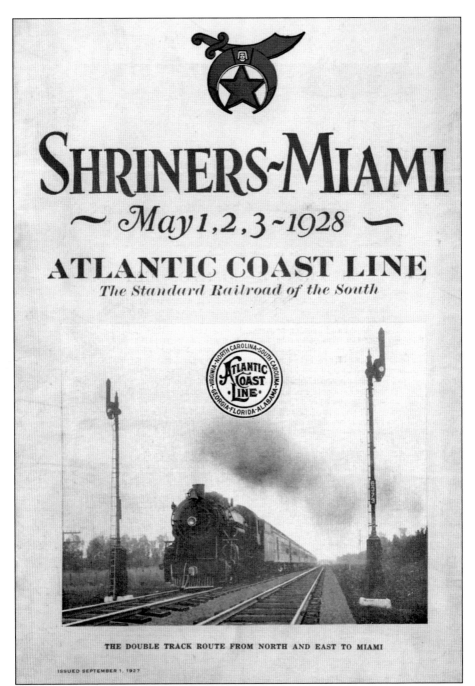

SHRINERS-MIAMI

~ *May 1, 2, 3 ~ 1928* ~

ATLANTIC COAST LINE

The Standard Railroad of the South

THE DOUBLE TRACK ROUTE FROM NORTH AND EAST TO MIAMI

ISSUED SEPTEMBER 1, 1927

In May 1928, the FEC was the host railroad for the first national convention ever to be held in Miami and, along with its longtime partner Atlantic Coast Line (ACL), made certain that the delegates' convention/vacation would begin the moment they boarded trains in their home cities. While FEC issued its own booklet for the convention—"Come on Fez, Miami Sez!"—the ACL also published a booklet that was distributed by passenger department representatives throughout its system. With 12 pages and two maps of Miami, the booklet made it almost impossible for Shriners to resist a trip to the Magic City.

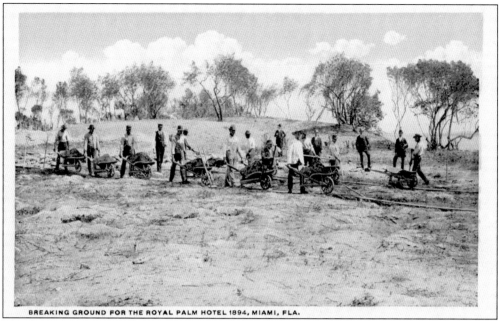

BREAKING GROUND FOR THE ROYAL PALM HOTEL 1894, MIAMI, FLA.

This famous image of the breaking of ground for the Royal Palm Hotel on the banks of the Miami River (seen at upper right) does not tell the whole story, for what occurred there was the destruction of a Tequesta burial mound and the subsequent scattering of the bones and artifacts that were buried within the mound. Standing in the background, behind the laborers, second from right, is Flagler's man in Miami, John Sewell, presiding over the event.

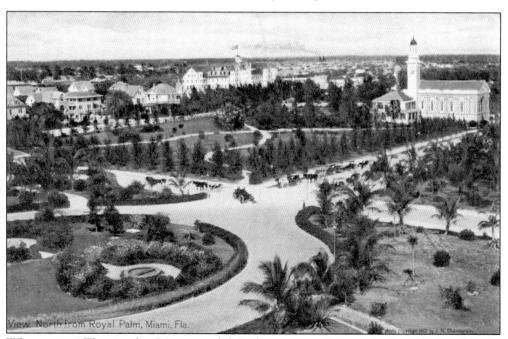

View North from Royal Palm, Miami, Fla.

What a view! The circular driveway at left is the entrance drive of the Royal Palm. Straight ahead in front of the camera is the Presbyterian church, and at left center is the Halcyon Hotel. Nothing showing in this view exists today.

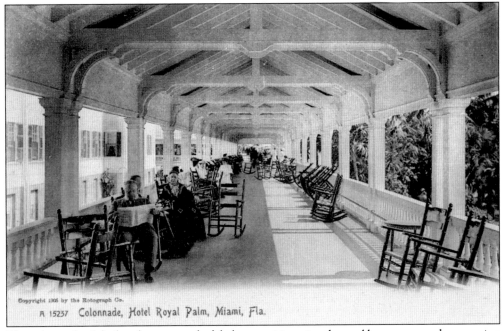

Copyright 1905 by the Rotograph Co.
A 15237 Colonnade, Hotel Royal Palm, Miami, Fla.

The colonnade of the hotel was a wonderful place to visit, enjoy the cool breezes, or read a magazine or newspaper. When the hotel was dismantled in 1930, several of the arches were removed, and they are still in existence in at least two Miami buildings.

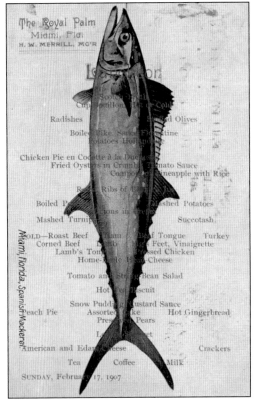

For whatever reason, Royal Palm menus seem to be the most difficult to obtain of any Flagler System/FEC Hotel Company hotel. This is the luncheon menu for Sunday, February 17, 1907, which the guests were able to use for a postcard. Among the delicacies offered, beef tongue, lamb's tongue, and homemade headcheese stand out.

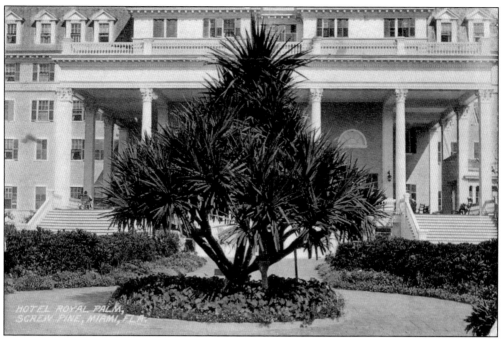

A close-up of the front of the hotel shows the verdant greenery that an arriving guest would gaze upon. It was a beautiful and welcoming entrance to Miami following the hack ride from the FEC station.

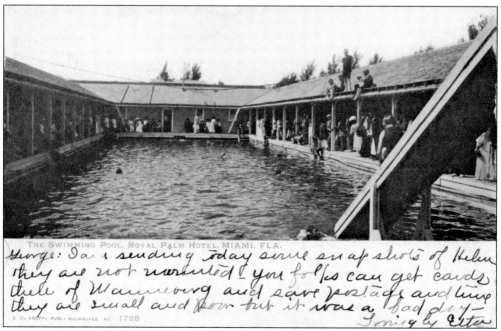

Always seeking goodwill in the communities it served, the Flagler Hotel Company, while closing the rest of the hotel for the summer, kept the swimming pool open and attended. Miamians delighted, both before and after the bridges to Miami Beach were opened, in enjoying the pool, the slide, and the leaps from the walkway roof into the clear, cool saltwater.

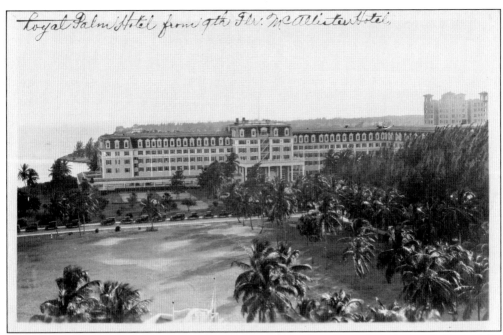

Royal Palm Hotel from 9th Flr. McAllister Hotel.

This expansive view shows the front of the hotel in all its glory. Seen from the ninth floor of the McAllister Hotel, the immensity of the property is evident. Within just a few years, the September 17–18, 1926, hurricane would spell the doom of the great hostelry.

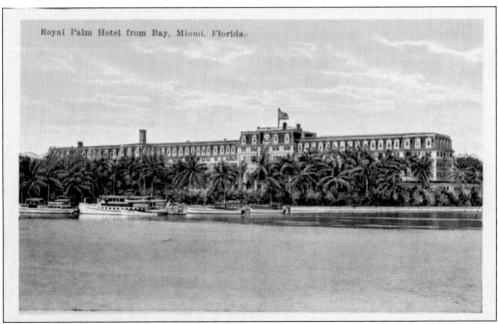

Royal Palm Hotel from Bay, Miami, Florida.

The rear view of the hotel, from the Brickell property on the south bank of the river, shows not only the hotel but also the yachts docked at the Royal Palm Marina, which remained in place for some years after the hotel was torn down in 1930.

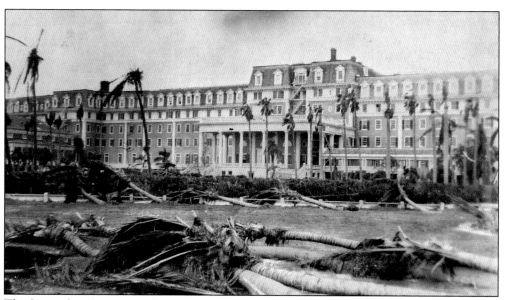

The September 17–18, 1926, hurricane brutalized a completely unprepared city, sparing nothing, including the Royal Palm, which was terribly damaged. Southeast Second Avenue was cut through the west end of the property, causing the loss of about one-quarter of the hotel; the hotel would reopen briefly in 1928, the coup de grâce administered in 1930 as the hotel was dismantled board by board, becoming only another wonderful Miami memory.

Miami Centennial '96
3500 Pan American Dr.
Miami, Florida 33133

Dear Friend,

Wonderful news! In honor of Miami's Centennial, I am re-opening the splendid Royal Palm Hotel on it's original site for one night only, February 24, 1996.

This grand gala is destined to be the Ball of the Century!

I am only inviting 1,000 of my closest friends. Space is very limited. Please do place your reservation now by calling the Miami Centennial office at 377-1996.

Can't wait to see you in your best formal "Gay 90's" attire.

Yours truly,

H M Flagler

Henry M. Flager

For the 1996 centennial, a great ball on the original site of the hotel was held under tents in the parking lots in front of the then-extant Dupont Plaza Hotel on February 24, 1996. Wearing period costumes, ball-goers celebrated the beginning of the five-month-long centennial, which climaxed with the arrival of the FEC display train at the original station site at Sixth Street and Biscayne Boulevard.

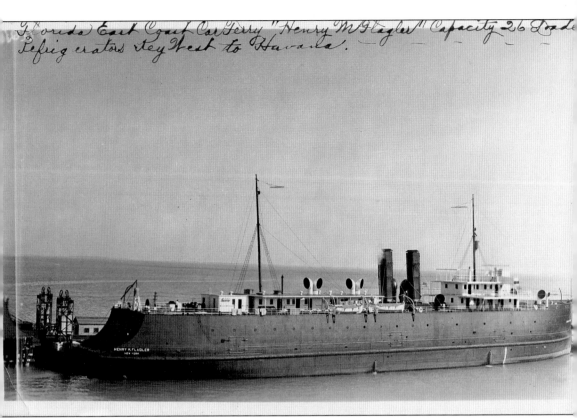

Florida East Coast Car Ferry "Henry M Flagler" Capacity 26 Loade *Refrigerators Key West to Havana.* —

The great Key West–Havana railroad car ferry *Henry M. Flagler* of the FEC Car Ferry Company would serve faithfully until the end of service brought about by Castro's Cuban revolution. With a capacity of 26 loaded freight or refrigerator cars, the *Flagler* is shown docked at Key West in December 1933.

Three

THE TIME OF THE TROLLEY

Unlike many places in America that had only electrically operated trolleys or streetcars, Miami's history is rich in the lore of the battery-powered streetcars, horse-drawn conveyances, and, of course, trolleys operated electrically, drawing their power from trolley poles and overhead wires. Though now making a return on rails in many American cities, with plans on the drawing board for that to happen in the Magic City, the demise of the streetcar should never have occurred.

With then-mayor Ev Sewell falling under the spell of the enticements being dangled by General Motors and the anti-rail conspiracy of the time, Sewell began a campaign decrying the electric cars as outmoded, noisy, and old-fashioned. In truth, the trolleys were none of those things, but in a city and a country being overwhelmed with propaganda espousing the internal combustion engine and the automobile as the best means of transportation, the pro-trolley people could do little more than stand by and wince painfully as a far quieter, more efficient, more economically sensible, and more viable mode of transport than the bus was coldly and calculatingly destroyed. In November 1940, the last Miami streetcar entered its barn at Southwest Second Street and Second Avenue for the last time, the time of the trolley, like so much else of Miami history, but a memory.

The first streetcar in the youthful city began operating in 1906. With a much too small ridership base, the enterprise lasted only a year and a half. Miami would not again see the streetcar until 1915, when a battery-powered trolley on rails operated into downtown from a point near where the Orange Bowl is today and then north on Avenue B (today's Northeast Second Avenue) to Thirty-sixth Street. By 1919, that operation was discontinued, and on January 7, 1922, the first actual streetcar using overhead wires since 1907 began Miami's electric railway era.

Because of the November 4, 1935, hurricane, Coral Gables trolleys, which came to downtown Miami via two separate routes, ceased operating. In 1939, streetcar service to Miami Beach via the County (now MacArthur) Causeway ended, and in November 1940, the time of the trolley came to an ignominious end, followed a day or two later by a parade of the then-new buses. Today, 66 years after that last streetcar ran, Miami is wisely planning the first of what hopefully will be a network of streetcar lines—now called light rail—for the Magic City.

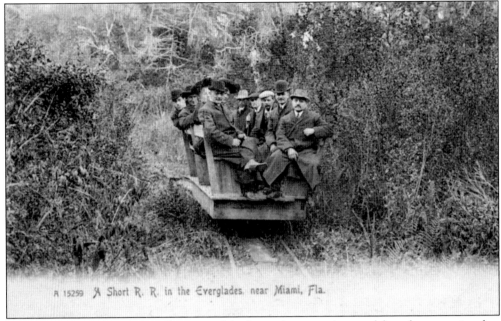

A 15259 A Short R. R. in the Everglades, near Miami, Fla.

Possibly the first of Miami's trolleys was of the horse-drawn variety, and for a few years, in what was then the Everglades, a horse-drawn vehicle on rails pulled tourists through the undergrowth to and from one of the two observation towers, each about 40 or 50 feet high, which provided visitors the opportunity to look out over the still undeveloped landscape.

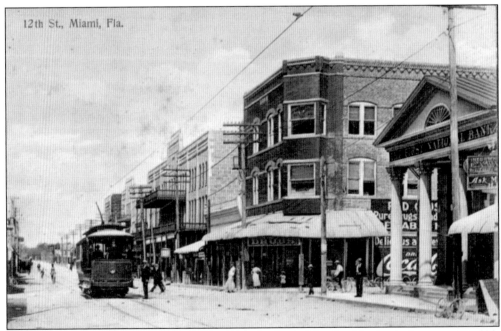

12th St., Miami, Fla.

The 1906–1907 electrically powered streetcar—this looks like Car No. 1—is shown on Twelfth (later Flagler) Street just west of First National Bank. Many of the buildings on the north (right) side of the street were still in place until the late 1960s.

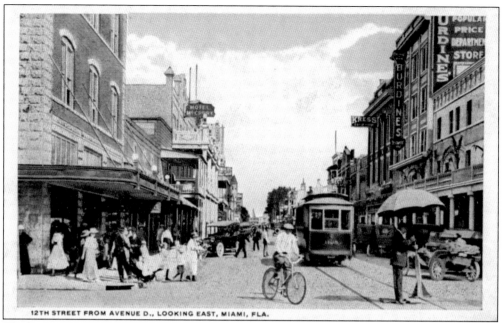

12TH STREET FROM AVENUE D., LOOKING EAST, MIAMI, FLA.

The battery car operation lasted from 1915 until 1919, and Car No. 1105 is shown here on Twelfth Street heading, we believe, west. The Hotel Biscayne is on the right and is shown on the cover and in the picture on pages 50 and 51. Burdine's and Kress are just east of the hotel, McCrory's is on the other (north) side of the street, and on the corner of Avenue D and Twelfth Street immediately to the left is Budge's hardware store.

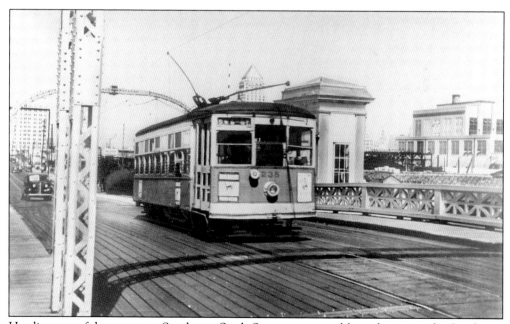

Heading out of downtown, a Southwest Sixth Street car is southbound crossing the Southwest Second Avenue bridge. The Dade County Courthouse looms over the center of the car, the Florida Power and Light Company building to the right.

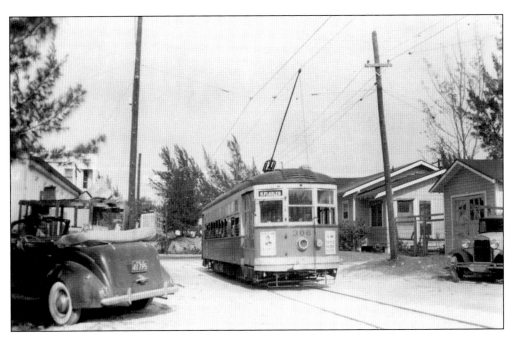

Once out of downtown and on the west side of the Miami River, the streetcars operated partly on Flagler Street and partly in the alley to the north of that street, which was known as the private right-of-way. Coral Gables cars, coming from the City Beautiful via Ponce de Leon, operated on their own trackage to Twenty-second Avenue, at which point they operated on the Miami company's tracks. Here No. 306 (top photograph) and No. 310, both ex–Miami Beach cars no longer operating across the County Causeway, are being used on the Miami lines in 1940 prior to the system's abandonment.

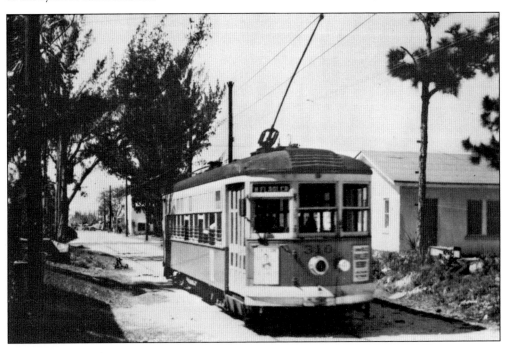

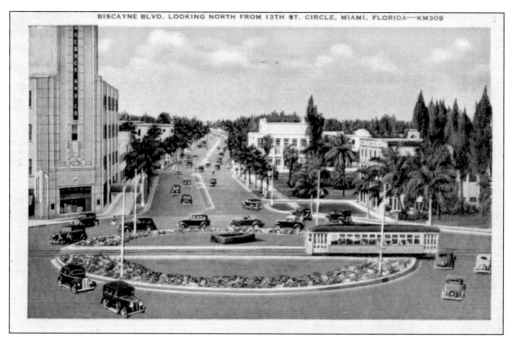

Shown just leaving the traffic circle on Biscayne Boulevard at Northeast Thirteenth Street, one of the big double-truck 300-series cars is two blocks from entering the County Causeway en route to Miami Beach. Had this service not ended in 1939, it would be one of the nation's foremost tourist attractions. The Sears Tower, partially visible on the left, is now the entrance to Miami's brand-new performing arts center.

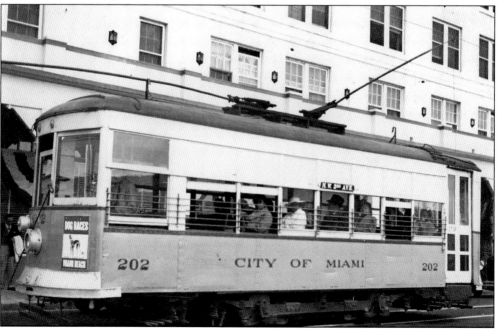

This single-truck Birney-type car is on the Northwest Third Avenue route. This is an extremely fine close-up view of the motorman's side of the car, by this time owned by the City of Miami but operated by the Miami Beach Railway Company.

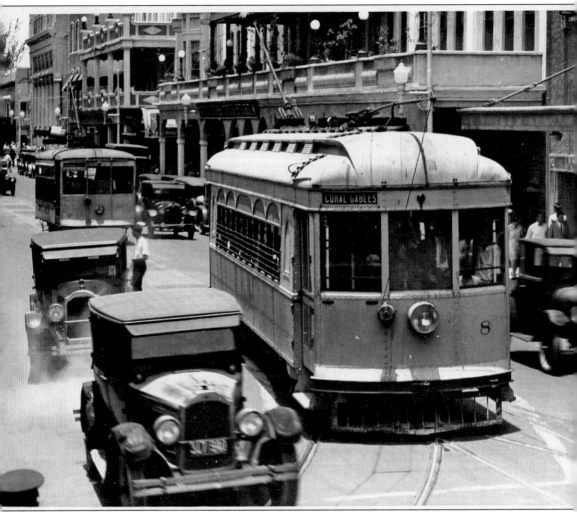

One of Miami's best-known photographs, this wonderful image was taken on Flagler Street at the point where the Coral Gables cars curved onto Southeast Second Avenue en route back to the Gables. What is incredible about this view, and what most people are not aware of, is that both of the streetcars are Coral Gables cars, No. 8 one of the high-speed interurbans that would come down Coral Way at close to 75 miles per hour and be in downtown Miami in 12 minutes, No. 107 one of the local cars that operated on Ponce de Leon in the Gables and then into downtown via Flagler Street, usually close to a one-hour trip.

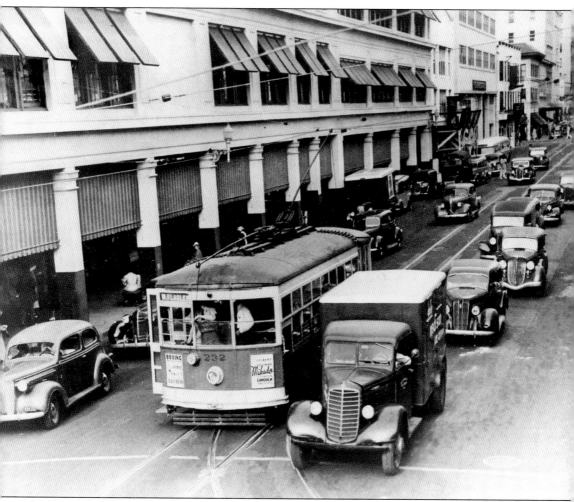

No. 232, operating as a Flagler Street car from downtown to Twenty-second Avenue and back, is shown here behind Burdine's on the Southwest First Street side as it pulls up for the light at Miami Avenue. Next to the streetcar, the Dolly Madison ice-cream truck also awaits the light. Both of the advertisements on the car in the *c.* 1938 view are for Miami Beach venues even though this particular car did not cross the causeway to the beach.

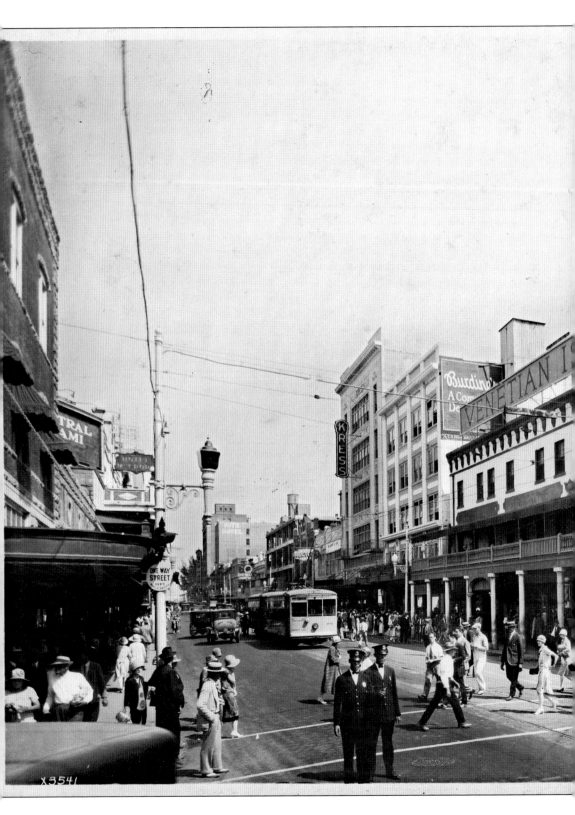

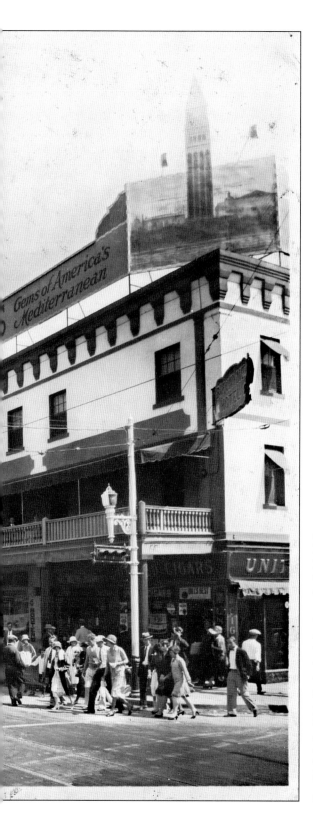

Although not overly changed physically from the earlier scene on page 45, this was a completely different city, throbbing with a new kind of life and ready to enter the greatest boom in its history. The Venetian Isles sign atop the Biscayne Hotel is an indication of the throbbing pulse of land sales that had already begun to envelop the entire area. The two streetcars in the middle of Flagler Street are Coral Gables cars, and they are packed with people heading for that city to look at George Merrick's property (See Images of America: *Coral Gables*). The street is thronged with "binder boys" hawking land that could be purchased for a "binder" of as little as $10. Those were incredible and exciting times!

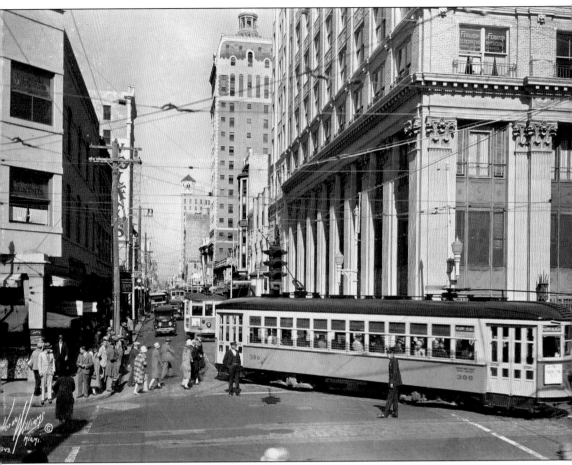

Miami Beach Railway Company No. 300 is signed for the island city as it makes the turn from
Flagler Street on to Northwest First Avenue en route to Miami Beach. The police officer appears
a bit perplexed as he looks at photographer Verne Williams; the man standing by the back door of
No. 300 seems completely nonplussed as the big double-trucker glides by him. City of Miami No.
220, signed for Buena Vista, prepares to move into the intersection. There are two more streetcars
in this view, one easily visible and the other one quite distant a good bit west on Flagler Street.

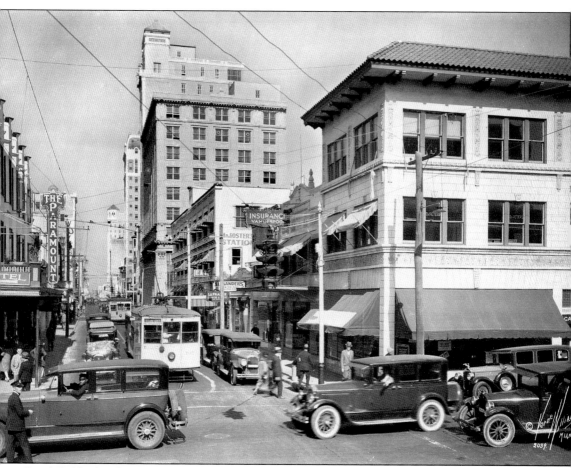

Coral Gables local car No. 107 is waiting for the light so it can make the right turn and begin the loop back out West Flagler Street to the Gables. Behind No. 107 is Miami No. 234. In this 1926–1927 view, note the number of fancy automobiles as well as the still-strong pedestrian traffic. This Williams photograph may have been taken just before the 1926 hurricane.

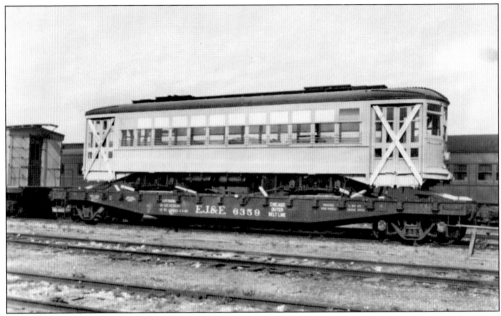

Once the trolley wires were taken down and streetcar service ended, most of the smaller cars were either scrapped or used for storage barns or in one case a paint shop and in another as a diner. Several of the big 300-series cars were shipped to St. Petersburg, where they spent their last years—until 1952—hard at work on Florida's last streetcar system.

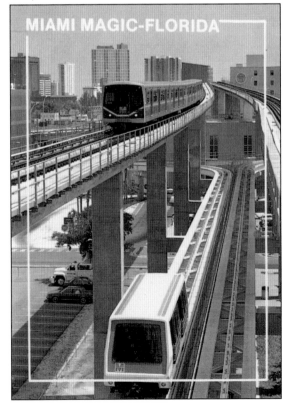

The return of what is called light rail to Miami has been preceded by both heavy rail and Metromover, the latter the electrically powered, operatorless small cars operating on a circulator loop in the downtown Miami area. The train on the left is today's third-rail-powered, electrically operated Metrorail system of today, with numerous extensions in the planning stages.

Four

A CITY BOOMS—AND THEN BUSTS

The Miami story, from its unlikely beginning through the current era, is completely unmatched by any other place in America and is more suited to a fable than to reality. Perhaps the most incredible part of the story is the great Florida boom of the 1920s, followed by the bust that began in 1926. Though devastating, the bust would lay the foundation for a more solid future.

Miami grew unceasingly almost from the moment of the arrival of the first train on April 22, 1896. People poured in from the United States and the Bahamas. George Merrick's family first came in 1898, and he developed Coral Gables after building many Miami subdivisions. Carl Fisher would come to Miami Beach—not yet named—in 1911. All of those arriving had one thing in common: they arrived on FEC Railway passenger trains at the Miami depot.

With the conclusion of the First World War, the pulse of business increased daily. New people meant new stores and new businesses, and while the black community grew larger in Overtown and the Jewish community opened more synagogues, people of every color and faith began the process of making Miami the melting pot it remains today.

The hottest commodity available was land, and the binder boys would turn over parcels of land and acreage 8 to 12 times in one day. Flagler Street and the other downtown streets and avenues became jumbles of yelling, screaming young men attempting to interest passersby in buying land. Subdivisions sprang up in all directions, and the Everglades were relentlessly pushed back. A new group of Miamians began to assume power, and people such as Marjory Stoneman Douglas; Frank Shutts, founder of the law firm of Shutts and Bowen and owner of the *Miami Herald*; Ev Sewell; James A. Cox, owner of the *Miami News*, formerly the *Metropolis*; Dr. Bowman Foster Ashe, first and longtime president of the University of Miami; aviation pioneer Glenn Curtiss and James A. Bright, partners in the founding of Hialeah, Miami Springs, and Opa-Locka; William J. Rubin and his son of Traveler's Luggage and Jewelry; Newt Roney, builder of Miami Beach's Roney Plaza; and D. A. Dorsey, the most prominent leader in the black community, started to exert influence in the growing city.

With the capsizing of the four-masted schooner *Prinz Valdemar*, blocking Miami's harbor entrance in January 1926, followed by the FEC's embargoing due to the immense and almost overpowering amount of freight that took up every single siding on the railroad between Jacksonville and Miami, and finally the September 17–18, 1926, hurricane, Miami's fate was sealed. Business would not recover until the late 1930s.

FLORIDA SOUVENIR

POST CARD

FOR COMMUNICATION THIS SPACE MAY BE USED. | THE ADDRESS ONLY TO BE WRITTEN HERE

STAMP

SOMETHING WORTH WHILE

In Order to Raise Quick Cash the Owners of

BISCAYNE HEIGHTS

Will sell 30 Nice Building Tracts, on, or close to Bay and One Splendid Eight Room House with Large Bay Front Lot, at

PUBLIC AUCTION, Tues., Feb. 22nd & Wed., Feb. 23rd

Sales open at 10:30 each morning on the grounds. Call early at

THE BISCAYNE HEIGHTS OFFICE, 235 12th St., next to First National Bank

for full information regarding this Sale, and secure Tickets   **ROUND TRIP FARE 25 Cts.**

"Something Worth While" was the opportunity to buy a lot or a house on the Bay (Biscayne Bay, of course) at Biscayne Heights, one of the innumerable developments that was giving everybody locally and throughout the country the opportunity to buy land or a building in Miami. This was just before the street and avenue numbering was changed in 1921, and what would become Flagler Street is still shown on the card as Twelfth Street.

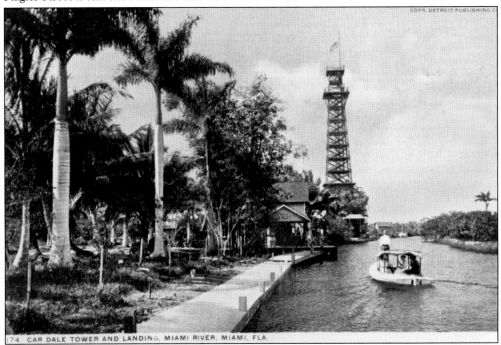

174 CAR DALE TOWER AND LANDING, MIAMI RIVER, MIAMI, FLA.

There were two towers on the Miami River, and both were tourist landmarks in the early years of the century and up until the mid-1920s. Here a small boat is approaching the Car Dale Tower and Landing.

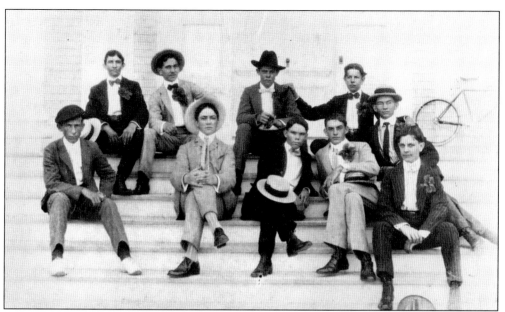

One of the most incredible Miami pictures ever taken, this image, like most in this book, has never before been published. It came from R. E. Coates, who sent it from Fort Meade, where he had moved and opened a business, in 1948. It was taken shortly after the First World War, and with the rumblings of the boom on the horizon, from left to right, Dexter Douglass, Dave Tuten, Monroe Padgett, Gus Haseltine, Fonnie Talbert, T. N. Gautier, John Gardner, Roddy Burdine, R. E. Coates, and Freman Burdine pose languorously on the steps of the Royal Palm Hotel.

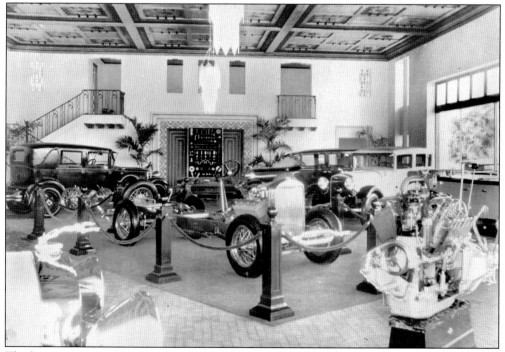

The boom was gaining strength as national automobile manufacturers licensed dealers in the Miami area. Shown here is what may be the first Dusenberg showroom in the city.

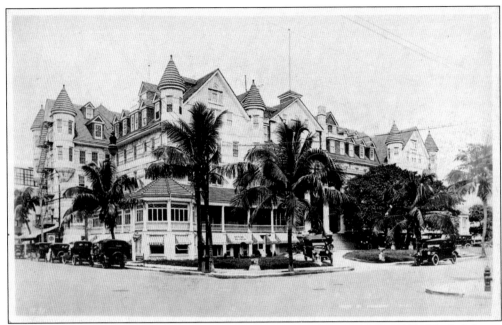

The Halcyon (sometimes called the Halcyon Hall) Hotel, at the corner of Twelfth (Flagler) Street and Avenue B (Northeast Second Avenue), was for several years Miami's second-largest hotel, outsized only by the Royal Palm. A much-beloved landmark of the early Miamians, it lasted until the late 1930s, when it was torn down to be replaced by the Alfred I. Dupont Building (see page 99), a monumental structure on the northwest corner of Flagler and Northeast Second Avenue. During World War II, the building would serve as the U.S. Navy District Headquarters. Both views show the hotel, but the photograph looking west on Flagler Street also shows the long-gone and lamented Hippodrome of Doc Baker (see page 97), along with one of Miami's earliest buses.

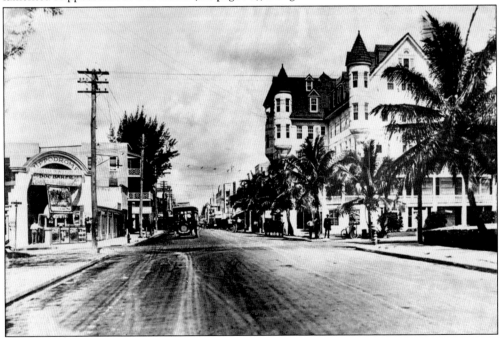

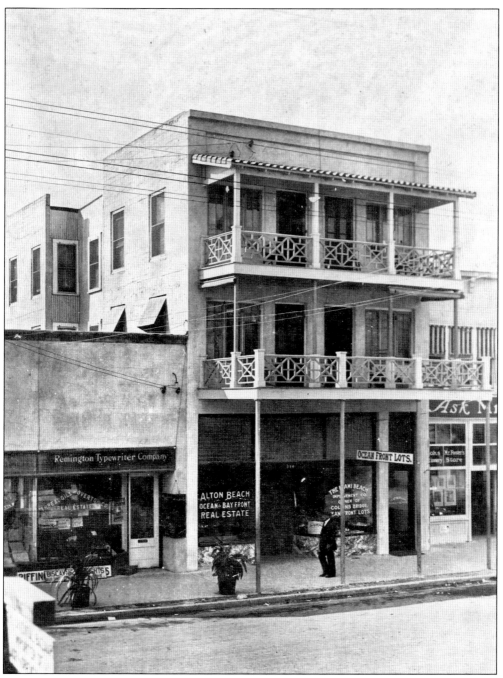

This stunning view is the Twelfth Street office of the Alton Beach Realty Company and the "Miami Beach Improvement Co. Owners of the Collins Bridge" (as it tells us on the right front window), both owned by Miami Beach's primary builder, Carl Fisher. The office on the right is the Ask Mr. Foster Travel Service, and on the left is, ostensibly, the Remington Typewriter Company storefront. A close look at the gold leaf on the window reveals that it is also, and by that time more importantly, the real-estate office of Threadgill and Overton Company; the sign on the sidewalk clearly tells us that they are selling Biscayne Heights property (see page 56).

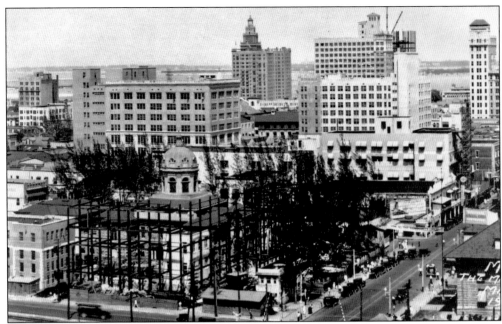

As the boom's momentum increased, the Dade County Courthouse was simply too small to handle the enormous crush of business. In this scene, the current courthouse is under construction, the steel framework being placed around the existing building. The street to the left is Avenue E (Northwest First Avenue), while Twelfth Street (Flagler) is to the right. The Everglades Hotel (center) has been completed, and other buildings are in various stages of construction.

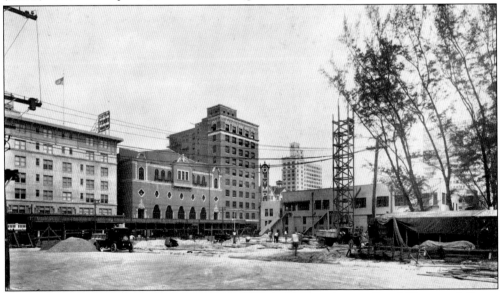

In this W. A. Fishbaugh photograph, the Ingraham Building at Avenue B and Thirteenth Street (Southeast Second Avenue and Southeast First Street) is under construction. Named for James E. Ingraham, for many years the Flagler System's land commissioner, the building would house all of the Flagler-related companies in Miami, with the FEC Railway's city ticket office on the first floor. Across the street is the sign of the just-completed Olympia Theater Building, today's Gusman Hall (see page 61).

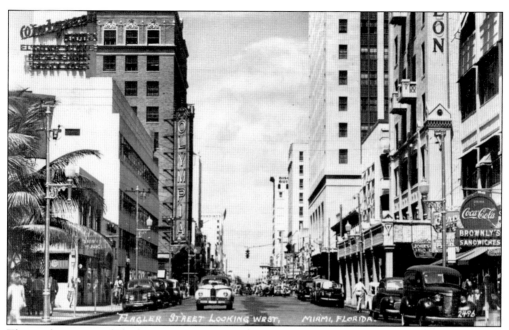

This striking view of Flagler Street, though a bit later than the time frame of this chapter, clearly shows the great sign of the Olympia Theater on the left, beyond the Walgreens Drugs building, whose sign is shown on top of the building.

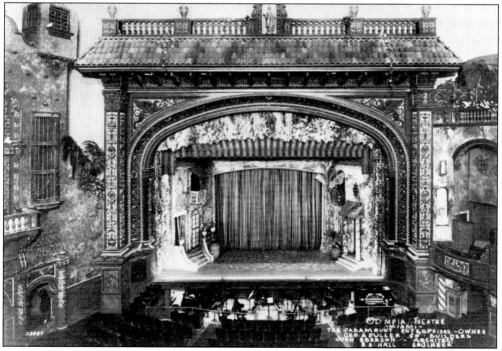

This is the original interior of the Olympia Theater. After years of neglect and concern that the building would be torn down, Miami industrialist Maurice Guzman stepped in and saved the facility, paying for the restoration that would bring this shining jewel back to prominence as a showplace of live theater for Miami.

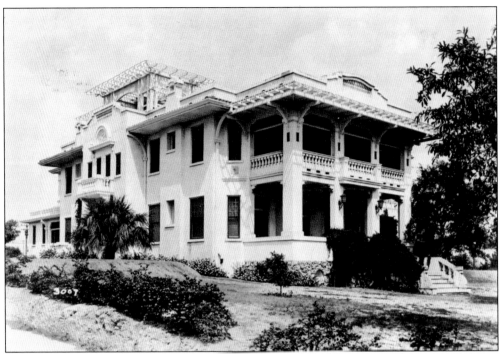

As the boom continued, fortunes were being made. This building at Northwest North River Drive and First Street was an example of the craftsmanship being put into the construction of buildings of all types.

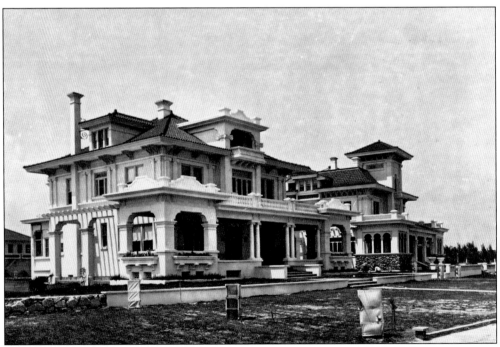

Two Miami homes are close to completion and ready for sale. It is believed that these two beautiful edifices were in the Point View section near Brickell Avenue and the Roads.

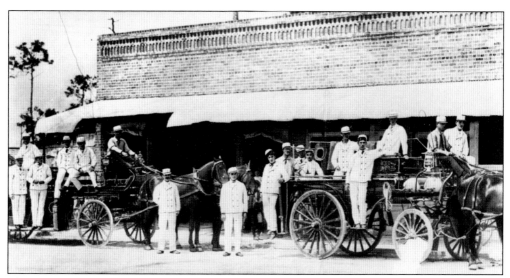

The last of Miami's horse-drawn fire units was retired just after World War I. Even though this view is somewhat earlier, we can still get an idea of the type of equipment that the fire department used at that time and the constraints in fighting fires that these units carried.

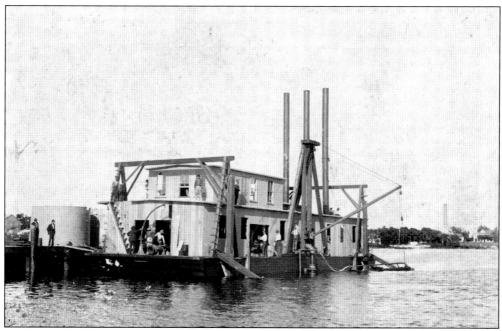

After World War I, with the tempo of business increasing and people pouring into the city, development and clearing of the Everglades began, assisted in no small way by dredges such as this, which would eventually deepen the Miami River and Biscayne Bay and destroy much of the mangrove growth that protected the "River of Grass."

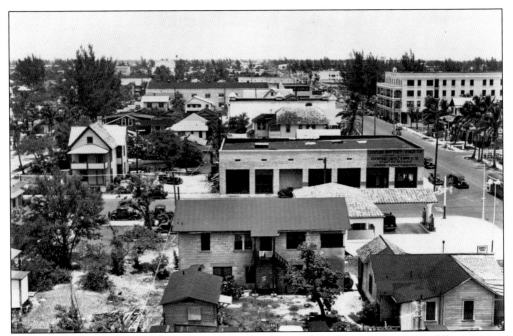

In the edge of the picture on the right is a Miami trolley, and the Clayton Battery and Engineering Company building is clearly seen right in the center. Behind Clayton is R. S. Evans Reo Cars. The Evans name is still a household Miami name, as his son, L. P., still has several Miami automobile dealerships.

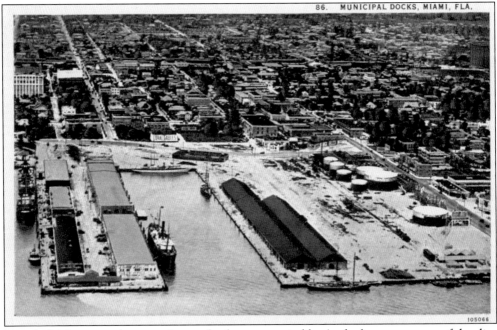

86.   MUNICIPAL DOCKS, MIAMI, FLA.

105066

To today's Miamians, this scene is completely unrecognizable. At the bottom are one of the slips and two of the piers for the old Port of Miami, fronting on Biscayne Boulevard from Northeast Sixth to Northeast Thirteenth Streets. At right are the Belcher Oil storage tanks, which fronted Thirteenth Street. They remained in place until I-395 was constructed through the area.

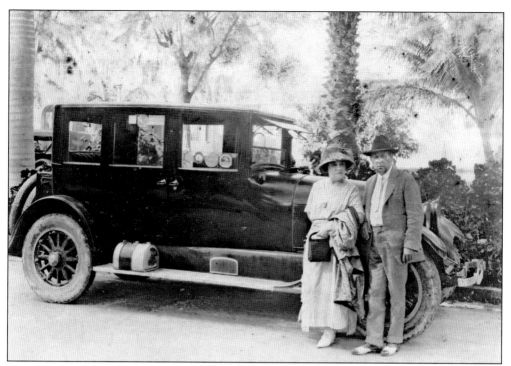

Miami pioneers Mr. and Mrs. Landon E. Edwards are shown in front of their car, which may be a Buick. Edwards owned a bookstore on Twelfth Street prior to the city's street renaming program.

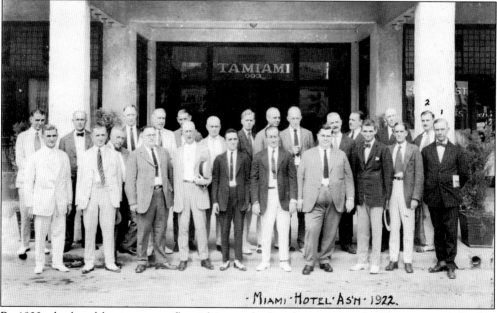

By 1922, the hotel business was flourishing and a hotel association had been started. In this very rare view, the organization is posing in front of the Tamiami Hotel. At far right in the front row is George McKinnon, president of the association and owner of the hotel bearing his name. Immediately behind him is Cliff Storm, vice president of the association and owner of the Tamiami, on whose steps the group is standing.

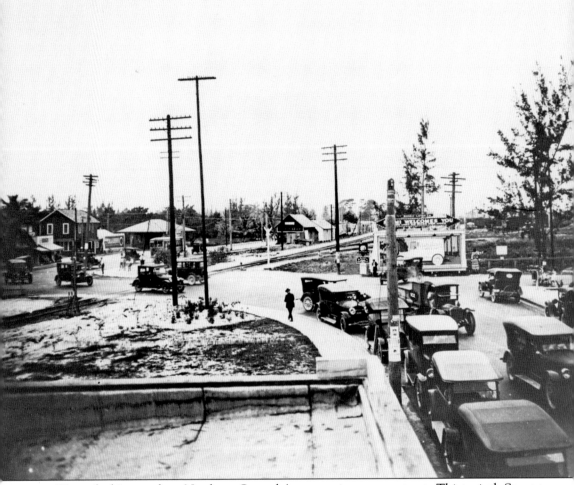

We are looking south on Northeast Second Avenue as it curves east onto Thirty-sixth Street to cross the FEC tracks and then curves south again heading for downtown Miami. This pre-1925 view includes, barely visible at left behind the telephone pole, a Miami trolley and, at right center next to the billboard, a Hialeah sign in the shape of a Seminole pointing west toward Hialeah. The FEC would build their Miami freight and passenger train yard in the open space to the right within two years. Though the vista has completely changed, the street still makes the same curve in the same place, and in many ways the intersection itself looks remarkably similar.

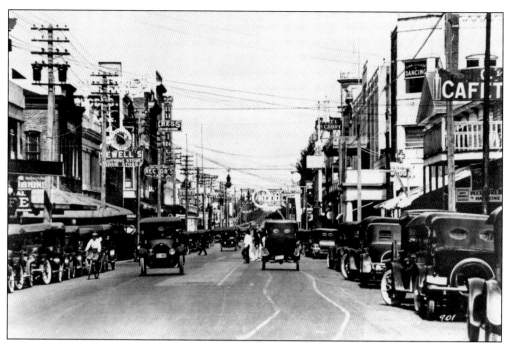

A marvelous early view shows Twelfth Street (Flagler Street) looking west from Avenue C (Northeast First Avenue). Sewell's, Miami's first store, is clearly visible on the left, behind which are Kress and Burdine's. On the right are McCrory's, the Hotel McCrory, and Western Union, and directly in the center, the FEC crossing gates are quite visible.

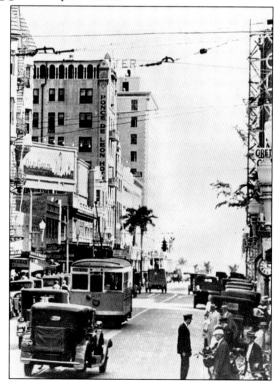

Several years later, the view is reversed and to the east, the Ponce de Leon Hotel is visible on the left, with the McAllister Hotel behind it. On the right is the Olympia Theater sign. Miami trolley No. 215 will shortly turn north on Northeast Second Avenue.

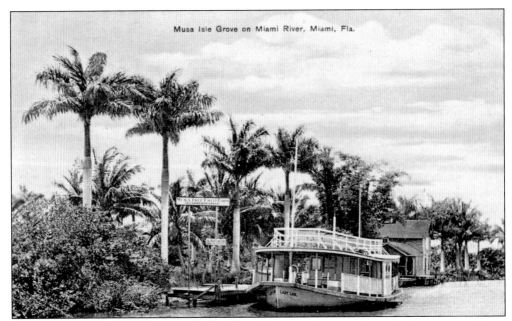

Musa Isle Grove on Miami River, Miami, Fla.

From Miami's earliest years, a trip up the Miami River by boat, a ride on the horse car to Musa Isle, and an enjoyable day at that famous attraction were something that all the tourists just had to do. The excursion boat *Lady Lou* is docked at the Musa Isle Fruit Farm/Richardson Grove dock while awaiting its next group of returning vacationers.

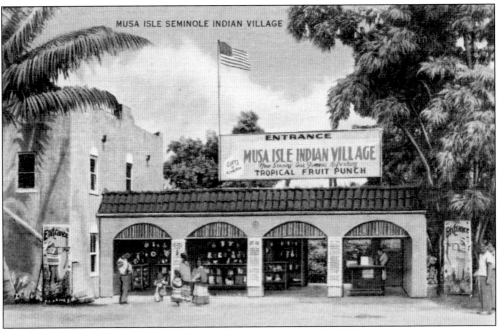

MUSA ISLE SEMINOLE INDIAN VILLAGE

At Northwest Twenty-seventh Avenue and Sixteenth Street, Musa Isle was the destination of choice for those wanting to see the brave Seminoles wrestle the alligators, and they were never disappointed. A Miami tourist attraction for close to six decades, changing tastes and increasing land values mandated the isle's closing and the sale of the property in the mid-1960s.

Everything in 1920s Miami was new or exciting! Prior to the building of the Rickenbacker Causeway to Key Biscayne, the Cape Florida Lighthouse was one of the less visited but always fascinating spots for adventuresome locals and tourists. Rich in South Florida history, this lighthouse is the revered focal point of Bill Baggs Cape Florida State Park.

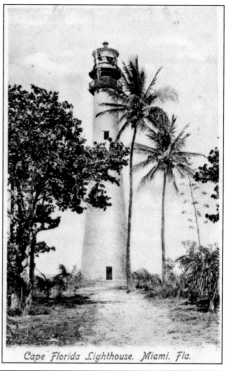

Cape Florida Lighthouse. Miami. Fla.

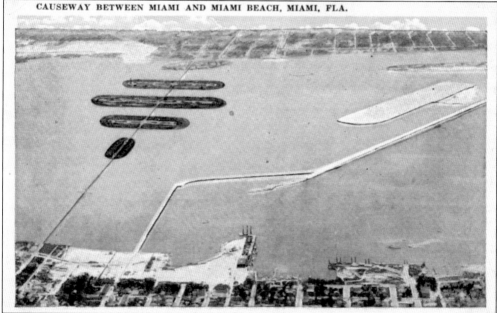

Carl Fisher built Miami Beach beginning in 1911; the only access to the island was first by water and then, from 1913 until 1920, via the wooden Collins Bridge, at the time the longest wooden bridge in the world. In 1920, the County Causeway opened, the Venetian Causeway following in 1925–1926. In this aerial view, the undeveloped causeway islands await planting and subdividing, and Watson Island, where the County Causeway curves to the right (lower left center), has not yet been filled in. The Miami port, along the lower Miami bayfront, is just being built.

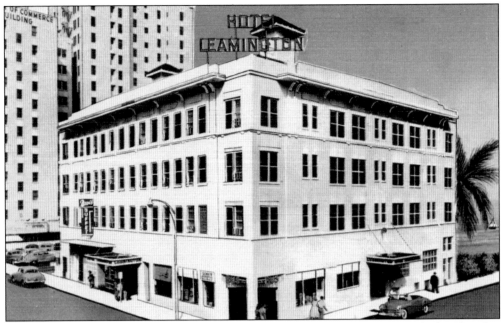

While shown later than the time frame of this chapter, the Hotel Leamington, with the Chamber of Commerce Building behind it, was a great gathering spot in the early and mid-1920s.

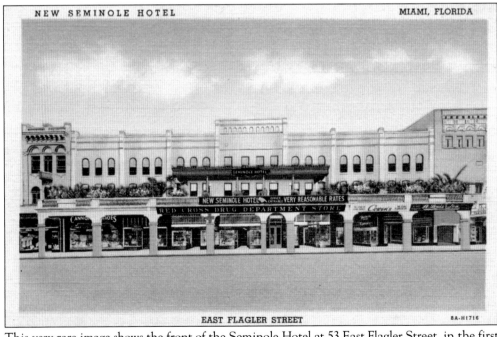

This very rare image shows the front of the Seminole Hotel at 53 East Flagler Street, in the first block east of Miami Avenue on the north side. For many years, Red Cross Drugs, a longtime favorite of early Miamians, occupied most of the ground floor of the building.

Cheesecake was as important to Miami as it was to Miami Beach, and in fact, Miami competed with the beach to display the beauties of the day. Whether showing off the winner of the 1926 Miss Miami Contest or using stunning bathing beauties in its 1920s "Miami By the Sea" booklets, Miami was no slouch in using the girls to entice vacationers to "the Land of Palms and Sunshine."

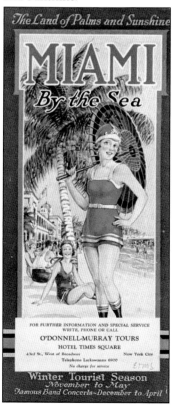

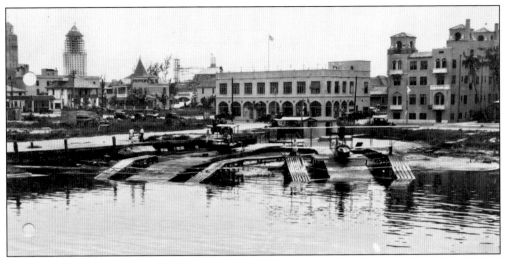

Among the sporting opportunities for the most adventuresome were those that involved going up in an airplane. Seen from the bay, the seaplanes of Rogers Air Lines await passengers at the foot of the Seventh Street anchorage. To the left, the Dade County Courthouse is nearing completion, and the Villa d'Este Hotel is at right. The Boulevard (later Biscayne Boulevard) is in front of the hotel and behind the planes.

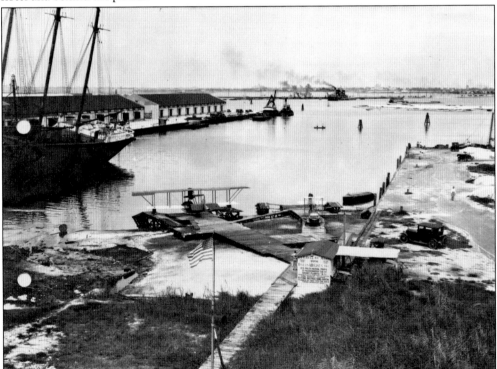

Stunning is an understatement for these images originally made for the FEC-owned P&O Steamship Company more than 80 years ago. This view looks east from the site that would, many years later, be an arena named for an airline, and in our vista is one of the schooners that brought freight into the city along with the County Causeway under construction in the middle and, far across the bay, Miami Beach.

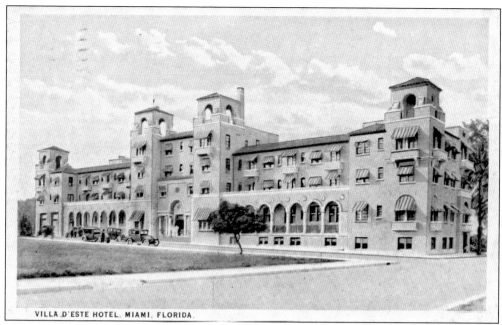

VILLA D'ESTE HOTEL, MIAMI, FLORIDA.

The corner of the Villa d'Este is shown in the upper photograph on page 72; the entire hotel is shown here. Built "uptown" at the time, the villa was, for no few years, considered one of Miami's finest early hotels.

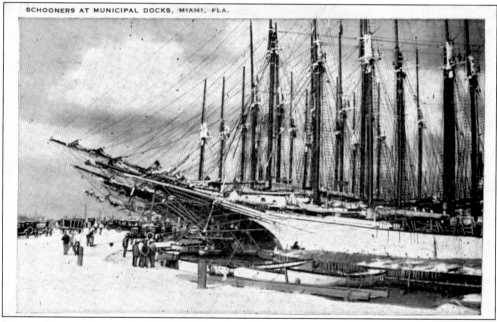

SCHOONERS AT MUNICIPAL DOCKS, MIAMI, FLA.

Due to the great boom, the FEC had been forced to mortgage itself, build new shops and yards, and double-track the railroad to handle the traffic. There was so much incoming freight that old four-masted sailing schooners were pressed into service as freighters. A group of them are shown here moored at the old port along the Boulevard. The *Prinz Valdemar* foundered at the mouth of the port's turning basin in early 1926, blocking the entrance for several months and forcing the FEC to embargo itself.

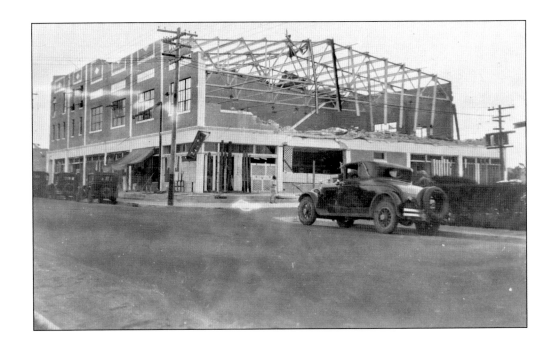

Until Hurricane Andrew in 1992, no hurricane devastated the area the way the September 17–18, 1926, hurricane did as it ripped through Miami and created havoc. While much has been written about that terrible storm, these photographs are from private collections, and the author believes that these particular views have never before been published. Both of these buildings were so brutalized that they had to be demolished after the storm.

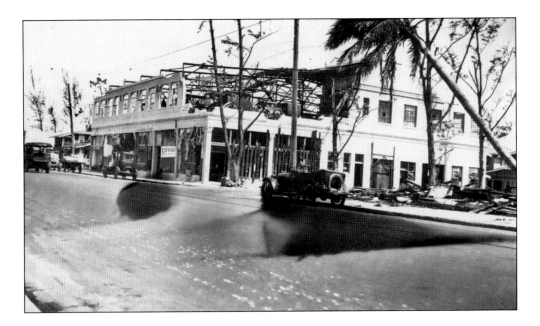

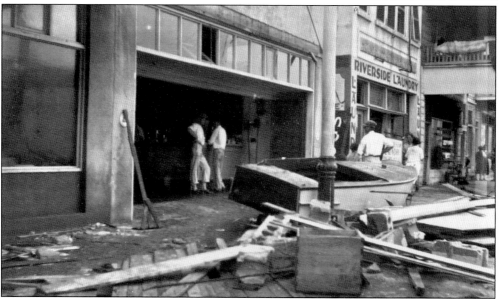

Although construction had been completed only months before the storm, the Meyer-Kiser Building was so badly damaged that top seven stories had to be removed following the hurricane. The Columbus Hotel, which survived the storm and stayed in business until the early 1990s, is shown on the right. A street scene in front of Riverside Laundry gives the reader a fine close-up view of what the storm wrought. Notice the small boat on the sidewalk in front of the store.

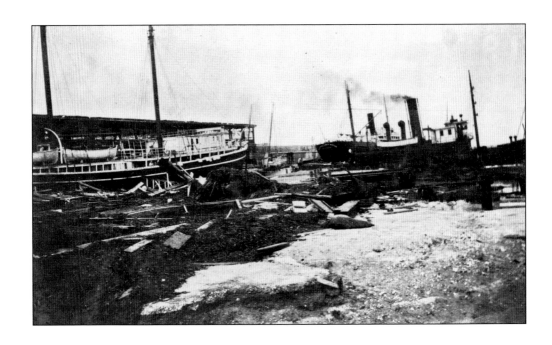

Ships were thrown out of water and dragged across the park and the Boulevard by the storm. These two visuals show boats grounded or so badly damaged that they could not be rebuilt.

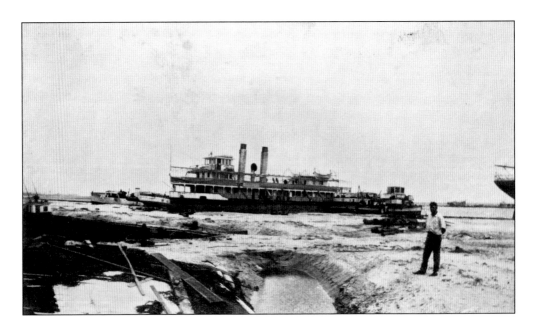

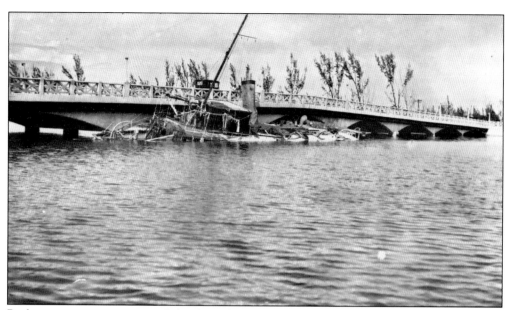

Bridges were not immune, and the ships that were thrown into them by the hurricane did no small amount of damage. Here a large trawler has been reduced to scrap by the force of the storm driving it into one of the newly built Venetian Causeway bridges.

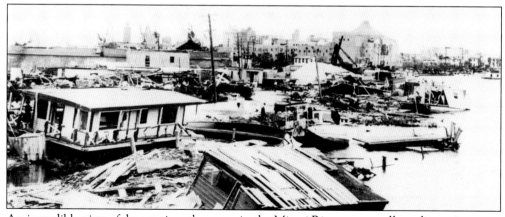

An incredible vista of devastation, the scene in the Miami River was equally as distressing as on the Boulevard. An untold amount of damage has been done in this scene looking east on the river toward downtown.

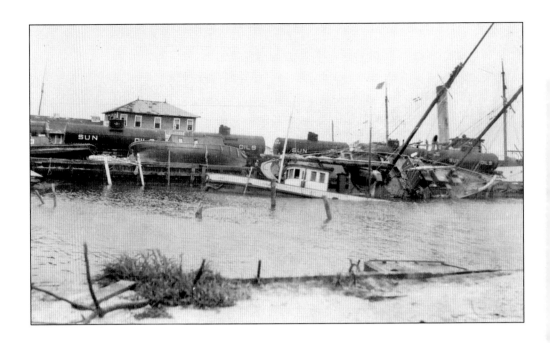

The scenes on the FEC Railway–P&O Steamship Company dock were pure chaos. From overturned freight cars to boats crushed and sunk against the south side of the dock, the damage was almost incalculable. The FEC/P&O station on the dock is shown in the center left background.

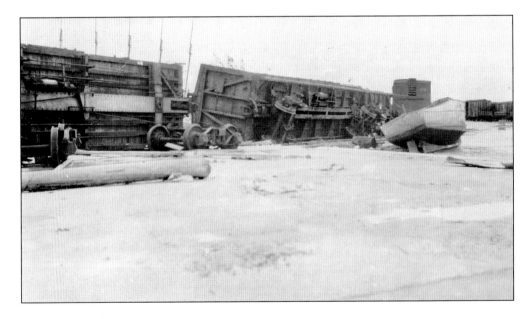

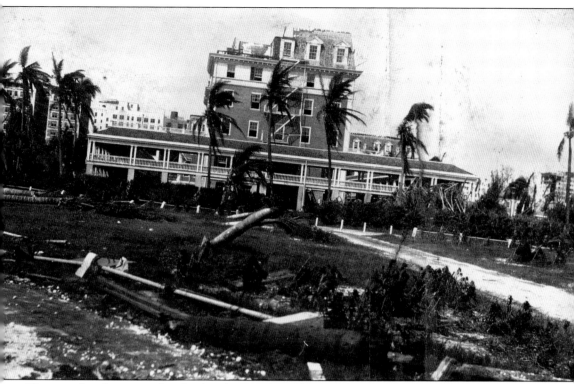

Photographs taken immediately after the storm would go into boxes or family albums, and many, if not most of them, have not survived other Miami storms, including the November 1935 and the 1947 hurricanes, as well as those that occurred later. From time to time, a surviving gem surfaces, and this great photograph, even though taped back together, borders on priceless, for it shows, from the east end looking west, the horrific damage that the Royal Palm Hotel suffered. The grounds were totally devastated, and the hotel was damaged almost beyond repair—note the upper floor on the left, where part of the dormer window has literally been removed. The hotel would open briefly for a few weeks in 1928 before being torn down, board by board, in 1930.

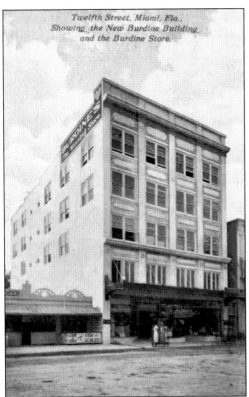

Twelfth Street, Miami, Fla.,
Showing the New Burdine Building
and the Burdine Store.

Even with all of the subsequent financial issues and problems caused by the events of 1926, Miami soldiered on, cutting its boundaries back from 121st Street to Eighty-seventh Street, where they remain today. Some businesses closed, but tourism proved to be the vital key that kept the city from falling into the depths of despair that affected manufacturing cities. Burdine's would remain a solid corporate citizen, and for many years, it was "The Winning Store!"

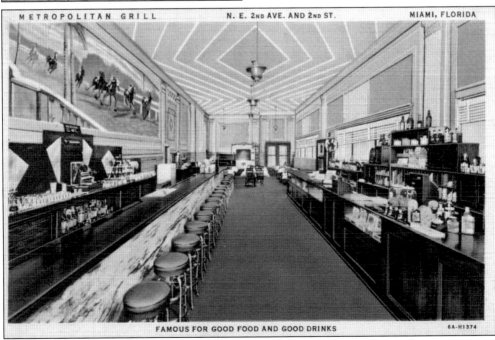

METROPOLITAN GRILL   N. E. 2ND AVE. AND 2ND ST.   MIAMI, FLORIDA

FAMOUS FOR GOOD FOOD AND GOOD DRINKS   6A-H1374

People continued to come, even though the bottom fell out for land sales, and restaurants and hotels adjusted their rates. The Metropolitan Grill, at Northeast Second Avenue and Second Street, remained "Famous for Good Food and Good Drinks."

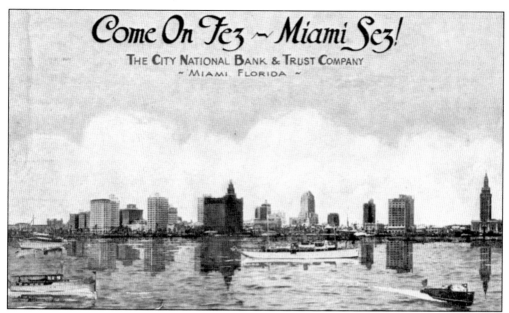

Miami continued to promote itself after the storm, and the efforts paid off handsomely when the city landed its first national convention—the Shrine—in 1928. Almost every business in the city contributed to the effort, and City National Bank and Trust sent out thousands of these postcards with the slogan initiated by the FEC Railway: "Come on Fez—Miami Sez!" The fez is the headpiece worn by Shriners.

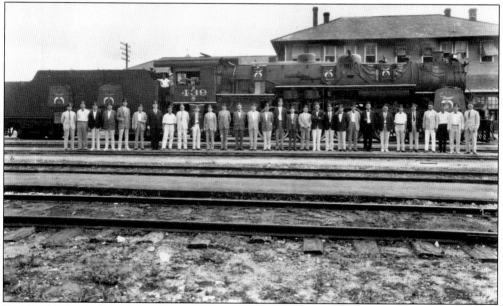

Besides the beautiful booklet issued by the FEC, the railroad published a series of photographs showing their Shriner employees standing next to one of their great 4-8-2 fast passenger locomotives at the Miami station. All of the men shown in this photograph were members of the Mahi (Miami) chapter of the Shrine, and it was in no small part thanks to the FEC's efforts that the Shrine was lured to Miami, coming from all over the country in innumerable special trains, which were parked on every available siding within the city.

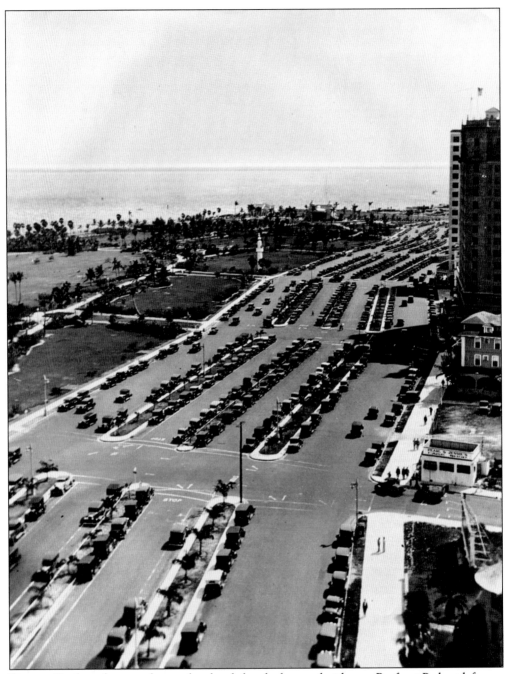

Biscayne Boulevard was newly completed and already thronged with cars. Bayfront Park, at left, was still beautiful and open, with only the bandshell at the south end in place. The spire in the center of the photograph was one of several placed along the Boulevard in honor of the Shrine.

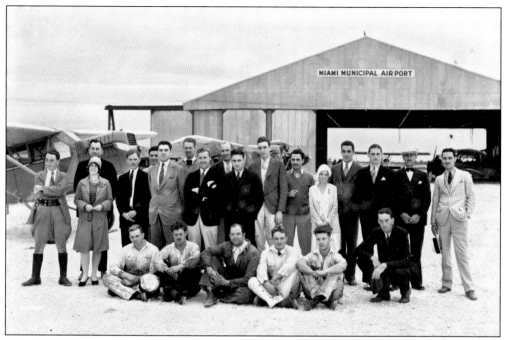

Aviation was becoming more commonplace in Miami. Miami Municipal Airport, on the site of today's Miami International, was quite a different place from today's immense facility. Mechanics, owners, pilots, and their friends are smiling brightly for a camera, recording a moment in time that is, today, hard to believe occurred.

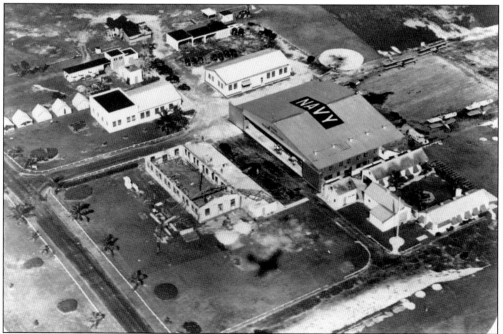

In Coconut Grove, adjacent to Dinner Key, the navy established an air station. The navy, and later the naval reserve, maintained a presence in the same location until the mid-1980s, although flights from there ended prior to World War II.

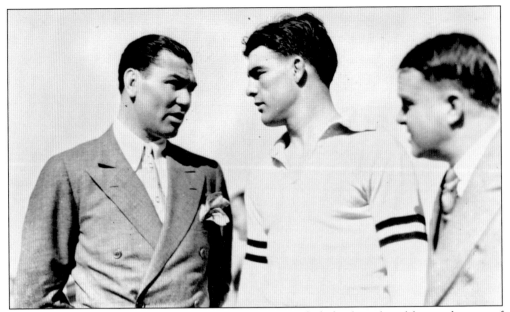

Even in the Depression, the city remained a magnet, particularly for the rich and famous, because of the magnificent weather that knew no economic troubles. Here the Manassas Mauler, Jack Dempsey, chats with two fans shortly after arriving at the FEC station. Dempsey fell in love with Miami and purchased the Vanderbilt Hotel on Miami Beach, renaming it the Dempsey-Vanderbilt.

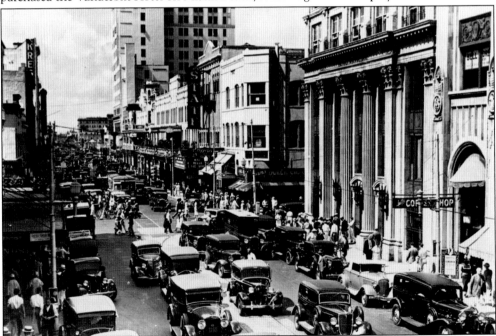

It's hard to believe that the city and the country were suffering through the worst economic times in history; in the 1935–1936 season, the FEC ran seven sections of the famous all-Pullman *Florida Special* on six different days and six sections of five different days, most other days that season requiring multiple sections also. In this early-1930s view, Flagler Street is thronged, and at the State Theater (on the right), the inimitable Mae West is starring in *Belle of the Nineties*.

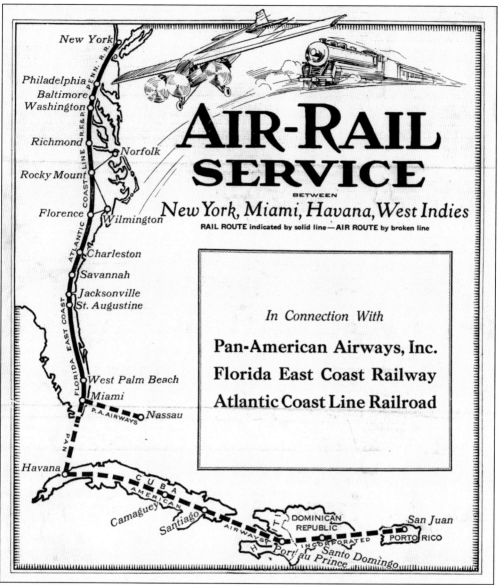

AIR-RAIL SERVICE

BETWEEN

New York, Miami, Havana, West Indies

RAIL ROUTE indicated by solid line — AIR ROUTE by broken line

In Connection With

Pan-American Airways, Inc.
Florida East Coast Railway
Atlantic Coast Line Railroad

Most airlines were initially funded and owned by railroads, Pan American being one of them. Initially backed by, among others, the FEC and ACL, Pan Am, in cooperation with the Pennsylvania, ACL, and FEC, inaugurated through rail-air service between Penn Station in New York City and Miami, where passengers where brought by luxury limousine to first Miami and then Dinner Key Seaplane Base, where they would fly to Nassau, Havana, other points in Cuba, Hispaniola, or San Juan. It was a glorious moment in time for American rail and air transportation.

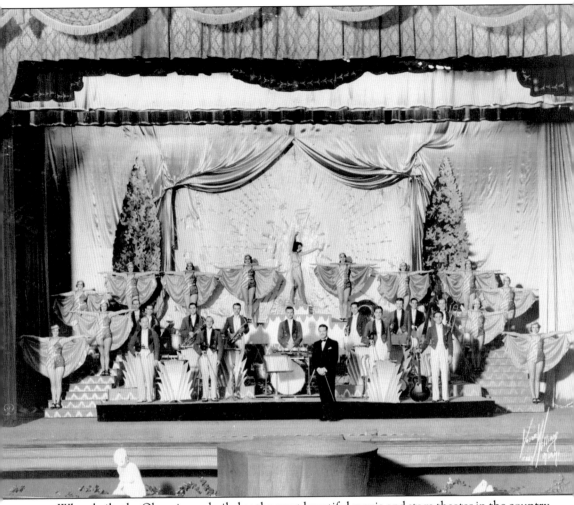

When built, the Olympia was hailed as the most beautiful movie and stage theater in the country, and indeed it was! Over the years, its glory faded, until, sometime in the early 1970s, Miami philanthropist Maurice Gusman donated the funds to restore the theater. Today operated by the city, it remains a Miami showpiece. In this marvelous 1932 photograph taken the evening of the theater's sixth-anniversary show and gala, orchestra leader Ray Teal stands in front of the group holding the baton. Regretfully, only a few of the musicians are identified: third from left in the second row, with the saxophone, is William "Sully" Sullivan; in the back, with the bass, is Orrin "Ab" MacDonell; and in the first row at far right, holding the guitar, is Andy Somma, whose family was well known in the restaurant business in Miami for many years. Leader Ray Teal would go on to national renown playing the sheriff in the *Bonanza* television series. (Courtesy collection of Gail and Mario Talucci.)

Five

STRUGGLING THROUGH THE DEPRESSION

They were hard times, and the cataclysmic occurrences of 1926 were harbingers of the Great Depression that would begin in the rest of the country in 1929.

Although the difficulties were not immediately evident, business following the 1926 hurricane began to spiral downward noticeably. Though events such as the 1928 Shrine Convention offered brief respites, the most visible business barometer was the number of FEC passenger trains operating into and out of the city, which declined beginning with the 1926–1927 season and did not increase again until the very late 1930s.

The Seaboard Railway arrived in 1925, the fabled *Orange Blossom Special* their premiere train, but, except for the line coming in from the west to their depot at 2206 Northwest Seventh Avenue, the right-of-way was so far west of the business and populated areas that the amount of traffic they carried, compared to the FEC, was minimal.

Banks began to close their doors, businesses small and large went under, hotels struggled to keep their doors open, and in 1931, the Florida East Coast Railway entered bankruptcy.

While it would certainly be a difficult era, the magic of the Magic City somehow prevailed, and with a seasonal service economy rather than a manufacturing economy to rely on, the effects of the Depression, while certainly not minimal, were nowhere near as severe as they were in the Northeast and the Midwest. Signs of recovery were evident as early as 1934, the 1935–1936 season being one of the busiest in FEC history. The railroad ran numerous additional sections of regularly scheduled trains on an almost daily basis from early December 1935 until mid-April 1936.

To no small extent, the effects of an art deco hotel construction boom on Miami Beach impacted Miami, as people found jobs on the beach and construction material companies had an outlet for their backlogged supplies. Little by little, business, while not rebounding, began to improve. By late 1938, there was a bright light at the end of the tunnel, and it was not, business-wise, an onrushing train.

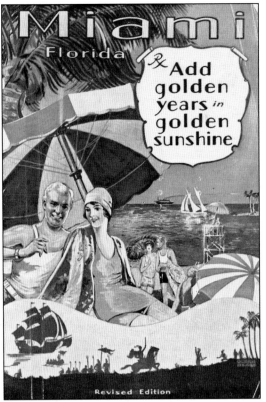

The 1930s began with a feeling of despair, yet the city attempted to put on a brave face in all of its advertising. The man under the umbrella has silver hair and the booklet is obviously directed to those a bit older than the youth-oriented pieces of the 1920s. The cover of this beautiful piece claims that by coming to Miami, you are given a prescription for adding golden years in golden sunshine.

Even with the economy in free-fall mode, Miami was still alluring to those who could afford to take advantage of the beauties of the city and the area, and the cruises to Nassau and Havana were the perfect thing to take one's mind off of the problems roiling the otherwise placid seas. Preparing to depart from the old port, a cruise passenger takes a last look at the Miami skyline, the Miami News Building directly over her right shoulder.

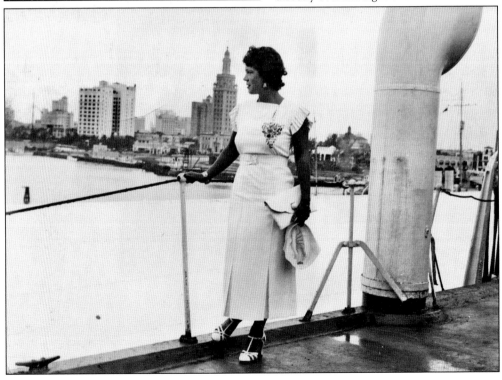

Following graduation from Miami High School on January 29, 1932, Harold Berke went to college and, following graduation, returned to Miami. He eventually opened Berke Displays, one of the most successful advertising/display firms in South Florida, whose catch phrase, "What the eye admires the heart desires," became a Miami byword. (Courtesy Mary Burke, Barbara Poliacoff, and Susan Frank.)

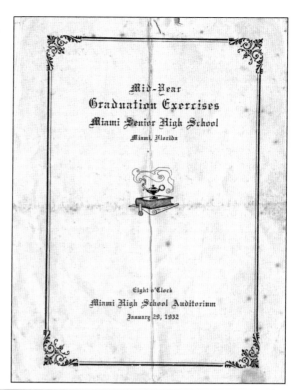

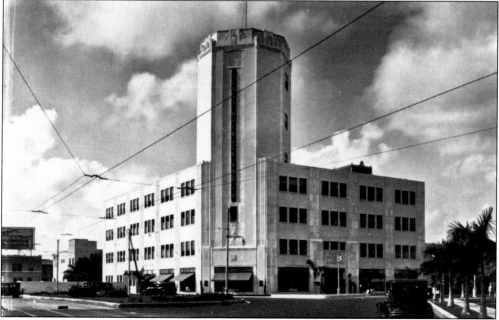

The Sears Tower, at Northeast Thirteenth Street and Biscayne Boulevard, now the entrance to Miami's Performing Arts Center, has been a city landmark for many years. This photograph, by the great Miami photoagrpher Calude Matlack, was taken on June 13, 1929, and shows the building with the trolley traffic circle in place but with business severely decreased, the street almost empty.

DIXIE DINNER CAFE
535. N. MIAMI AVE. 537
HATCH BROS., PROPS.

Soup, 15c.; with Order, 10c.

Regular Dinner	.55	Roast Chicken (Half)	.80
Dixie Vegetable Dinner	.60	Fried Chicken (Half)	1.00
Dixie Plate Lunch	.50	Dixie Chicken Buisects	.75
		Chicken Ala King	.65
Chicken Fried Steak	.45		
Minte Steak	.55	Mashed Potatoes	.10
Sirloin Steak	.90	Mashed Potatoes Cream Gravy	.15
T. Bone Steak	1.15	Hash Brown Potatoes	.20
		Plain Fried Potatoes	.15
Roast Beef	.45	Creamed Potatoes	.25
Roast Pork	.50	Au Gratin	.30
Pork Chops	.50	French Fried	.15
Veal Cutlets (Breaded)	.50	Lyonnaise	.20
Lamb Chops	.70		
		Plain Omelet	.30
Bacon and Eggs	.45	Ham Omelet	.45
Ham and Eggs	.45	Cheese Omelet	.45
Two Eggs (Any Style)	.30	Tomato Omelet	.40
Boiled Ham	.30	Jelly Omelet	.45
Bacon	.30		
Country Sausage	.50	Hot Roast Beef Sandwich	.25
		Egg Sandwich	.15
Wheat Cakes and Syrup	.20	Ham Sandwich	.15
with Coffee	.25	Bacon Sandwich	.15
Mothers Oats with Cream	.20	Chicken Sandwich	.25
Corn Flakes with Cream	.20		
Stewed Prunes	.10	Cheese Sandwich	.15
Grape Fruit (Half)	.10	Dixie Special	.25
		Western Sandwich	.30
Buttered Toast	.15		
Milk Toast	.25	Fruit Salad	.25
Plain Toast	.10	Dixie Combination	.40
Bread. Butter, Coffee	.15	Potato Salad	.20
Doughnuts (Three)	.10	Chicken Salad	.40
Rolls or Cake	.10	Tomato and Lettuce	.40
Pork and Beans	.40	Fried Trout	.45
Side Order	.15	Baked Red Snapper	.50
Ham and Cabbage	.45		
Corn Beef and Cabbage	.45	Oyster Stew	.40
		Fried Oysters (Half)	.50
Bread and Butter	.10		
Hot Biscuits (Two)	.10	Pies (All Kinds)	.10
Dixie Corn Cake	.10	Coffee (None Better)	.05
Baked Apple	.15	Tea (Pot to Order)	.10
with Cream	.25	Iced Tea (Special)	.15
Puddings	.10		

See other side for Specials.

As the Depression deepened and business continued to decline in the early years of the 1930s, menu prices dropped almost precipitously. The Dixie Dinner Café at 535 and 537 North Miami Avenue was, by 1932, offering T-bone steak at $1.15 as the most expensive item on their menu. Harlis, with two locations and claiming to be always open, would not survive the debacle.

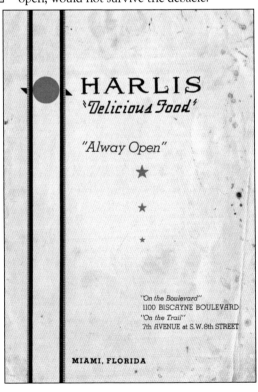

HARLIS
"Delicious Food"

"Alway Open"

★

★

★

"On the Boulevard"
1100 BISCAYNE BOULEVARD
"On the Trail"
7th AVENUE at S.W. 8th STREET

MIAMI, FLORIDA

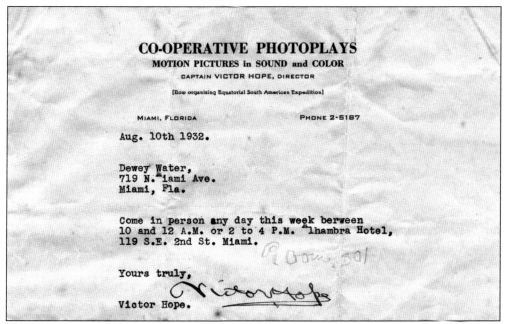

Even many Miami historians are completely unaware that, in the 1920s, Miami had a budding and active movie industry with dreams of supplanting Hollywood. With the Depression, it would never be, and anything that remains from the companies that were located in the Magic City is gold to collectors. Here Victor Hope, owner of the soon-to-disappear Co-Operative Photoplays, is asking Dewey Water to join him at the Alhambra Hotel in downtown Miami for a meeting.

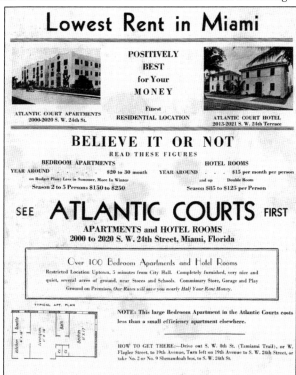

Rents during the 1930s declined to a level that seems almost incomprehensible today. The Atlantic Courts, at 2000 Southwest Twenty-fourth Street, advertised the lowest rent in Miami, with hotel rooms for $15 per month if rented on a yearly basis.

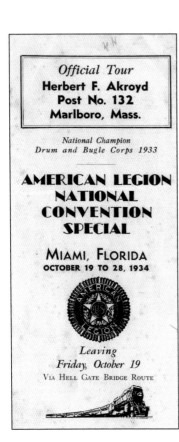

Struggling though the city was, the chamber of commerce was relentless in pursuit of conventions and other business that would increase business and lift sagging spirits. Through dogged persistence and cooperation with the city's convention bureau, the American Legion chose Miami for its 1934 conclave. Though the official convention dates were from October 22 through 25, the special trains bringing Legionnaires from all over the country would leave their home cities three and four days early in order for the conventioneers to begin celebrating the moment they boarded their trains.

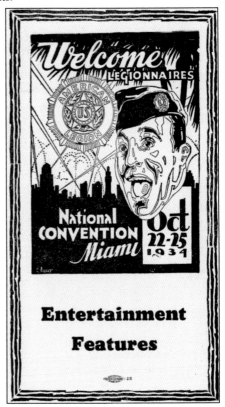

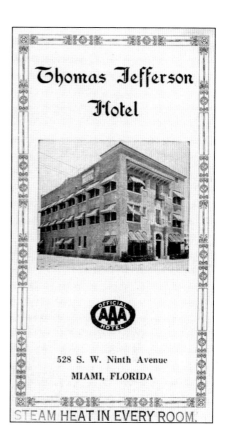

Thomas Jefferson Hotel

OFFICIAL AAA HOTEL

528 S. W. Ninth Avenue

MIAMI, FLORIDA

STEAM HEAT IN EVERY ROOM.

The Thomas Jefferson and the Howell were two of the hotels in the near southwest section of the city that were struggling to stay afloat. The Jefferson Hotel brochure shows rates as low as $1.50 per day, and although the Howell's brochure does not include a tariff, it is safe to say that their rates were not much more than those shown on the flyer for the Atlantic Courts on page 91 or those of the Jefferson. Both hotels are in the area that became known as Little Havana, today a major tourist attraction and the center of activity for Miami's Cuban community.

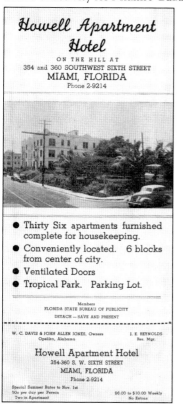

Howell Apartment Hotel

ON THE HILL AT
354 and 360 SOUTHWEST SIXTH STREET
MIAMI, FLORIDA
Phone 2-9214

- Thirty Six apartments furnished complete for housekeeping.
- Conveniently located. 6 blocks from center of city.
- Ventilated Doors
- Tropical Park. Parking Lot.

Members
FLORIDA STATE BUREAU OF PUBLICITY
DETACH — SAVE AND PRESENT

W. C. DAVIS & JOHN ALLEN JONES, Owners   I. E. REYNOLDS
Opelika, Alabama   Res. Mgr.

Howell Apartment Hotel
354-360 S. W. SIXTH STREET
MIAMI, FLORIDA
Phone 2-9214

Special Summer Rates to Nov. 1st
50c per day per Person $6.00 to $10.00 Weekly
Two in Apartment   No Extras

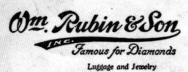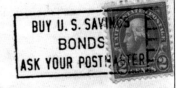

Wm. Rubin & Son
INC.
Famous for Diamonds
Luggage and Jewelry
31 NORTH MIAMI AVENUE
MIAMI, FLORIDA

MIAMI, FLA.
NOV 2
10:00PM
1938

BUY U.S. SAVINGS
BONDS
ASK YOUR POSTMASTER

Mrs. Ellen Harris
113 Shoreland Arcade
Miami, Florida.

In the 1926 John B. Gordon Patrol/Miami Chapter of the Ku Klux Klan booklet issued for the Klonvocation in Washington, D.C., there are advertisements for, among others, Coca-Cola, Florida Power and Light, and Traveler's Luggage and Jewelry on Miami Avenue, with William Rubin and Son, Proprietor, Jewish KKK Headquarters. Apparently, the Miami Klan at that time was more of a social organization than anything else, although it is quite likely that blacks were not welcome as members.

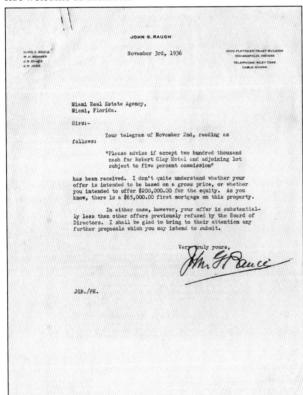

This November 3, 1936, letter, in which John G. Rauch of Indianapolis is offering $200,000 for the Robert Clay Hotel and adjoining lot, is fascinating and shows that, even in the worst of times, people with money still have money. The offer was subsequently rejected, but this is one of the few pieces known to still exist that directly makes a cash offer for a Miami property during the Depression.

94

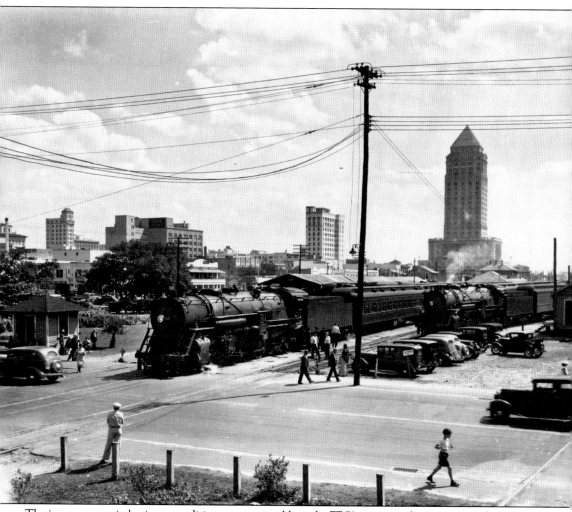

The improvement in business conditions was noticeable as the FEC's passenger business strengthened. This photograph was shot by FEC Railway Company photographer Harry M. Wolfe, and in it two passenger trains await departure from the downtown Miami station, the roof of which is visible at center right. The street in front of the camera is Northwest Fifth Street, and the view is southeast. The tall building at right center is the Dade County Courthouse, and nothing else in the photograph looks the same today. The FEC's passenger trains are but a memory and Miami's Metrorail rapid-transit trains run on an elevated right-of-way above where the tracks are shown. It was a very special moment in time.

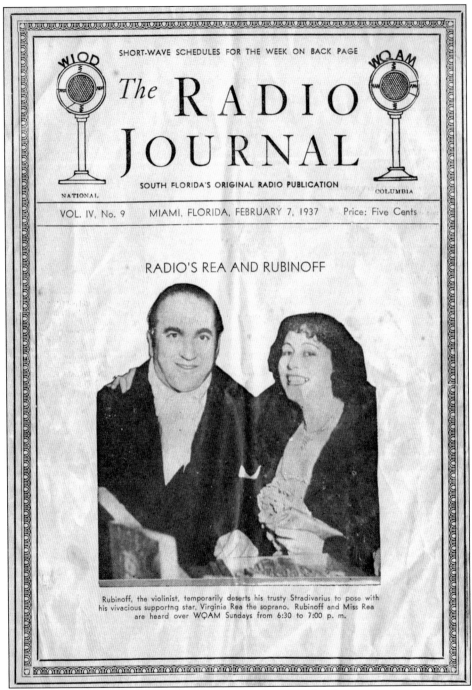

SHORT-WAVE SCHEDULES FOR THE WEEK ON BACK PAGE

The RADIO JOURNAL

SOUTH FLORIDA'S ORIGINAL RADIO PUBLICATION

NATIONAL

COLUMBIA

VOL. IV, No. 9   MIAMI, FLORIDA, FEBRUARY 7, 1937   Price: Five Cents

RADIO'S REA AND RUBINOFF

Rubinoff, the violinist, temporarily deserts his trusty Stradivarius to pose with his vivacious supporting star, Virginia Rea the soprano. Rubinoff and Miss Rea are heard over WQAM Sundays from 6:30 to 7:00 p. m.

The Radio Journal is one of those never-before-seen rarities that brings absolute joy to Miami memorabilia collectors, and this is the February 7, 1937, edition. Issued by radio stations WIOD (Wonderful Isle of Dreams) and WQAM (Florida's first radio station), the 12 pages are loaded with advertisements, photographs of radio celebrities, and, of course, the schedules of the two stations that sponsored this publication. In 45 years of collecting Miami memorabilia, this is the first of these the author has seen. (Courtesy collection of Gail and Mario Talucci.)

The Hippodrome (shown previously on page 58) remained, until the block was demolished sometime in the early 1950s, a favorite Miami watering hole and attraction. The 1937–1938 menu puts on a cheery face as the Depression decade begins to wind down.

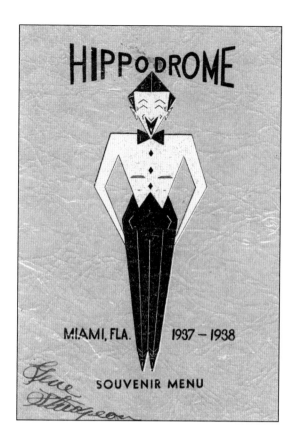

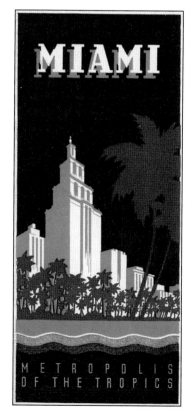

The art deco look, an appearance of streamlining and moving forward, is evident on the cover of this 1938–1939 promotional booklet titled "Miami: Metropolis of the Tropics," which features, naturally, the wonderful weather as well as the innumerable activities available to the visitor.

respectfully dedicated to his honor
The Mayor of Miami

Bayfront Park Gold and Silver Shell

march

by

Joseph La Monaca

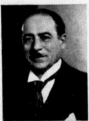

JOSEPH LA MONACA

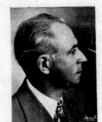

CEASAR LA MONACA

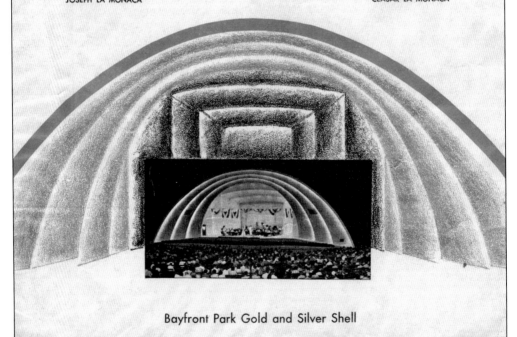

Bayfront Park Gold and Silver Shell

Miami's three most prominent musicians during the 1930s and for some years later were Mana Zucca, Orrin "Ab" MacDonell, and Caesar La Monaca, all of whom were famed for their concerts and their contributions to Miami's musical history. La Monaca, for years, gave regular free concerts in the Bayfront Park Bandshell, shown here on the cover of the "Bayfront Park Gold and Silver Shell March" music sheet, written by Joseph La Monaca and dedicated to Miami mayor Everest "Ev" Sewell.

Indicative of the growing optimism of the very late 1930s was the announcement by Edward Ball, chairman of the Florida DuPont Estate, that he would build a magnificent new office building on the site of the Halcyon Hotel to be named the Alfred I. DuPont Building, complete with ground-floor banking facilities for Ball's Florida National Bank. It was a major shot in the arm for a city just beginning to regain its confidence.

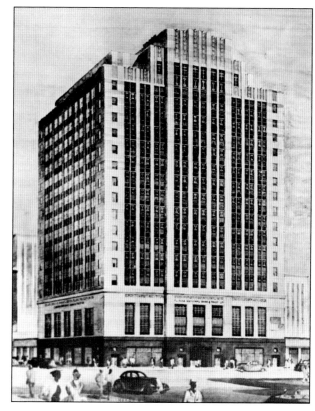

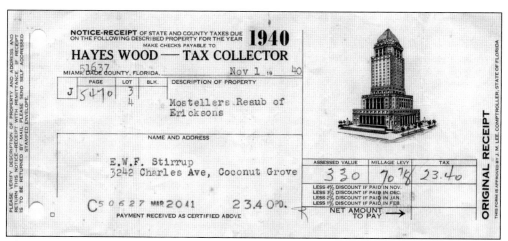

The Stirrup family was one of Coconut Grove's pioneer black families, records indicating they arrived there around 1890; they are still members of the community. This 1940 tax receipt shows that E. W. F. Stirrup paid taxes on one of his Grove properties that year in the amount of $23.40.

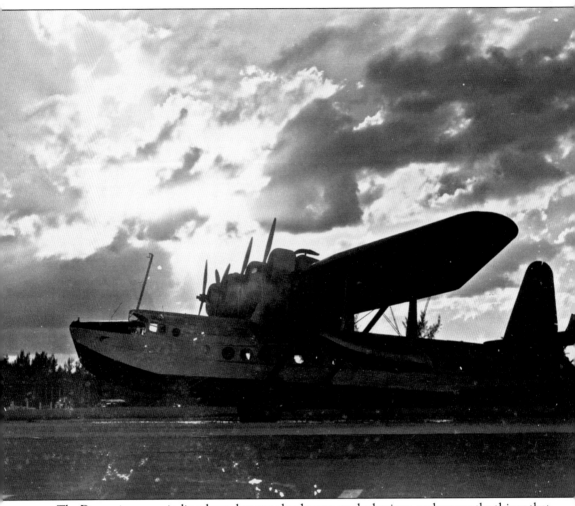

The Depression was winding down, but war clouds were on the horizon, and among the things that would be lost forever with the coming of war was the end of service of one of the most romantic chapters in the history of aviation, Pan American's fabled "Flying Clippers," which operated from Dinner Key, using what is now Miami's city hall as their office, base, and airport. It is twilight and the last flight has been towed ashore, the Clipper era sadly ended. With a prophetic mood of sunset melancholy and impending darkness, the plane is moved toward its hangar for the last time, suggesting the darkest of nights into which, at the end of day, all things must go.

Six

WORLD WAR II AND ITS AFTERMATH

With the onset of war, Miami was no different than the rest of the country, except that four out of every five Army Air Corps fliers trained on Miami Beach, coming into Miami for the most part on FEC and Seaboard trains. Most people are not aware that Miami was, in its own right, a major military center, being headquarters for the navy's Caribbean and South Atlantic Command, the home of a navy subchaser school, a major WAVES training center, a naval gunners school, and the home of the Coast Guard's Southern Command.

Although not within the city limits, Richmond, in south Dade County, became a major airship base. Northwest Dade and Opa Locka hosted both a marine air station and a navy air station. The Coast Guard ensconced itself in a base at the mouth of Government Cut where the ocean meets the ship channel on the Miami Beach side. German POW camps were established in several locations throughout Greater Miami.

Just as with Miami Beach, the military—in Miami's case, the navy and the Coast Guard rather than the army—essentially took over the city. FEC and Seaboard trains operated non-stop, section after section bringing thousands of new recruits to town and introducing them to Miami's winter weather. All buildings along Biscayne Bay were required to have shades closed at night, and just as on the beach, cars were driven at night with hooded headlights to protect against German subs attacking allied ships, which could be silhouetted against the city's lights.

Everybody did their part, and soldiers and sailors were warmly welcomed. While sacrifices by the civilian population were great, the war gave businesses a much-needed shot in the arm, and the ending of the war saw a much different Miami than the city that had gone into the war in December 1941. Within just a few years, Miami would be almost unrecognizable to the old-timers as thousands of service men who had gotten sand in their shoes during their Miami-based training returned with their wives and families to build a new life in the Magic City and its environs.

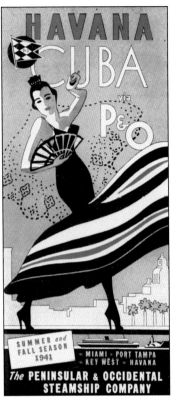

The 1941 season would be the last until after the war for the P&O Steamship Company. The SS *Florida*, like the FEC Car Ferry Company's boats, was pressed into government service. All of the ships survived the war, following which they were returned to their civilian roles. The P&O would not return to either Port Tampa or Key West, instead operating three days a week from Miami to Havana, returning the next day. After a brief attempt to build a Miami-Nassau business following the communist takeover in Cuba, the P&O found it could not compete with the newer and larger ships of the late 1960s.

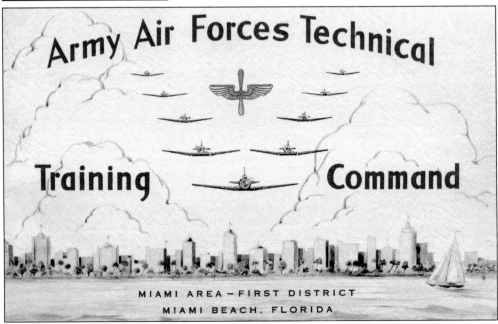

Although the Army Air Forces Technical Training Command did most of the actual training on Miami Beach, it was the First District of the Miami Area, which covered a large part of South Florida. While many pictures show activities on Miami Beach, several show the boys detraining and then carrying out further duties in Miami.

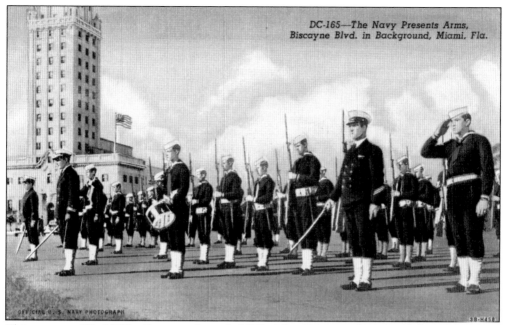

This very rare World War II postcard is titled "The Navy Presents Arms" and shows a group of cadets drilling on Biscayne Boulevard with the Miami News Tower in the background.

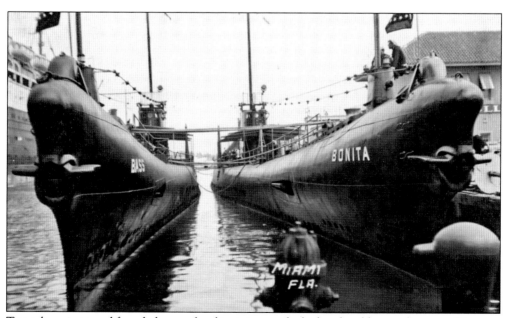

Two submarines used for subchaser school training are docked at the old port adjacent to Biscayne Boulevard. During the war, all manner of naval vessels were literally close enough to downtown and the Boulevard to reach out and touch.

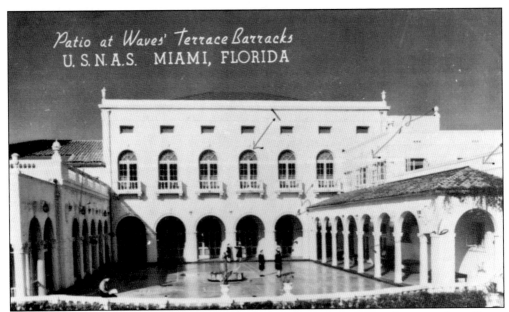

Patio at Waves' Terrace Barracks
U. S. N. A. S. MIAMI, FLORIDA

While Miami itself is often overshadowed by the later historical interest shown in the military on Miami Beach, which is a function only of the publicity that the Army Air Force received, the lack of attention given to the work of the Women's Naval Corps—the WAVES—borders on shameful. Here several WAVES chat on the patio of the Terrace Barracks, the main Miami housing facility for them.

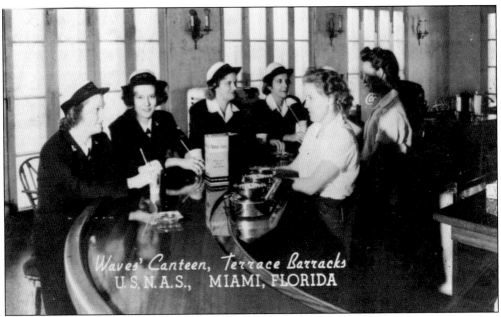

Waves' Canteen, Terrace Barracks
U. S. N. A. S., MIAMI, FLORIDA

Taking a break in the Terrace Barracks canteen, five WAVES are attended by two female bartenders. All of the women—as well as the men—were welcome at the various USO and community canteen facilities operated by Miamians and beachites on both sides of the bay.

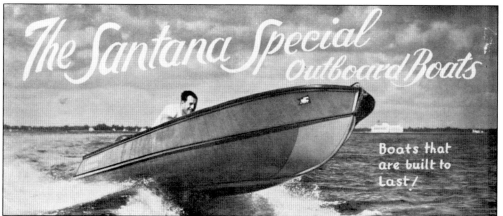

The Santana Special Outboard Boats

Boats that are built to Last!

With the ending of hostilities, Miami began to return to normal, and people who had been forced to do without and avoid unnecessary travel began to loosen up. Such luxuries as speedboats once again became easily accessible to the average person, and one could purchase a Santana Special Outboard from Santana Marine Service at Dinner Key. For those of more modest means, a ride on one of the Miss Miami Speed Boats, operating from Pier 5 1/2 at the Miami City Yacht Basin was within the budget.

MIAMI CHAMBER OF COMMERCE
MIAMI, FLORIDA

"MISS MIAMI SPEED BOATS"

"Established 1929"

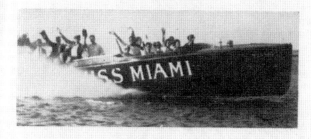

The Only Speed Boats Operating in Miami

ORIGINAL VENETIAN ISLANDS
SIGHTSEEING TRIP

PIER 5½

Miami City Yacht Basin

This Trip is not a tiresome one, but timed just right for your enjoyment.
Boats Depart at Regular Intervals.

●

BOATS AND PILOTS
Lncensed Under
U.S. Gov't Inspection
CAPT. GENE APEL, SR.

PHONES
2-9883
3-4968

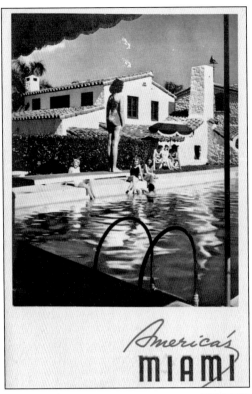

America's
MIAMI

After the war, Miami's publicity people, while still using the "Magic City" tagline, began referring to the city as "America's Miami," and this beautiful, all-color booklet was one of the first to do away entirely with black and white as a photographic advertising medium. However, very little had changed for the black population, and the housing situation was worsening, so much so that in 1951 the University of Miami published this booklet, "Negro Housing in the Miami Area," which was a much-quoted academic study of the issues and problems Miami's blacks were facing.

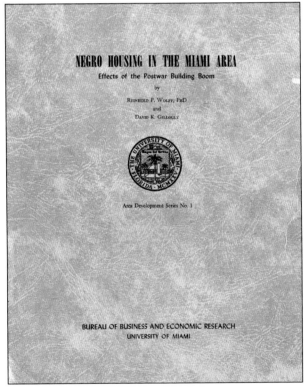

NEGRO HOUSING IN THE MIAMI AREA

Effects of the Postwar Building Boom

by

REINHOLD P. WOLFF, PhD
and
DAVID K. GILLOGLY

Area Development Series No. 1

BUREAU OF BUSINESS AND ECONOMIC RESEARCH
UNIVERSITY OF MIAMI

Prior to the destruction of Miami's bayfront by the building of the ill-advised Miamarina and the Rouse Company's Bayside development, Pier 5 was one of the world's great fishing destinations. People came from all over the world to board "The World's Finest Fishing Fleet." The huge sailfish and sign were Miami landmarks until destroyed by progress.

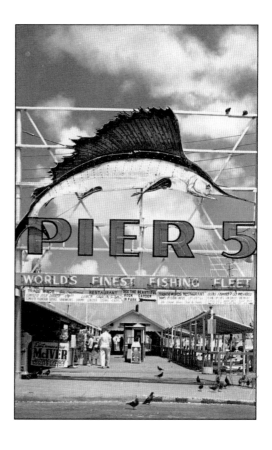

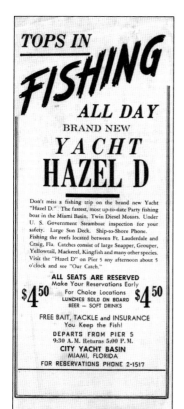

One of the boats based at Pier 5 was the *Hazel D*, brand-new at the time this flyer was published around 1948. Bait, tackle, and insurance were included in the $4.50 price, and "You keep the Fish!"

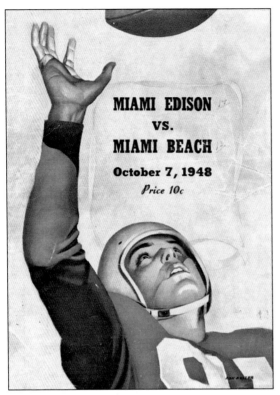

MIAMI EDISON
vs.
MIAMI BEACH

October 7, 1948

Price 10c

After the war, there was once again time for high school sports, and for many years, Miami boasted five great high schools within city limits: Miami High, Miami Edison, Miami Jackson, Booker T. Washington, and Tech High. On October 7, 1948, Edison was matched against its cross-bay rival, the always-scrappy Miami Beach High, and the following year on November 7, Jackson played Landon of Jacksonville in the Orange Bowl. Because there were at that time only six public high schools in the county, teams came in from much of the state to compete with the Miami gridders.

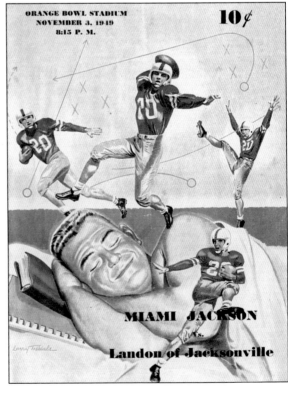

ORANGE BOWL STADIUM
NOVEMBER 3, 1949
8:15 P. M.

10¢

MIAMI JACKSON
vs.
Landon of Jacksonville

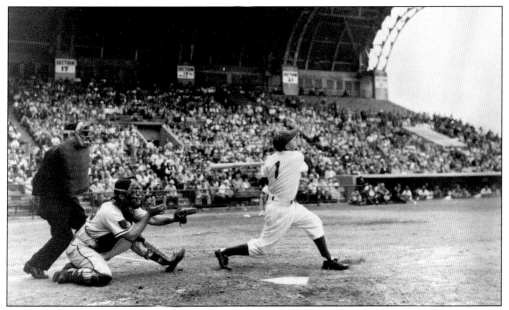

With a new boom beginning, there were more and more opportunities for leisure and recreation. During spring training, major-league baseball exhibitions were a regular pastime for the partisans of that sport. Shown here at Miami Stadium, a Brooklyn Dodger has connected against the old Milwaukee Braves. That was a long time ago!

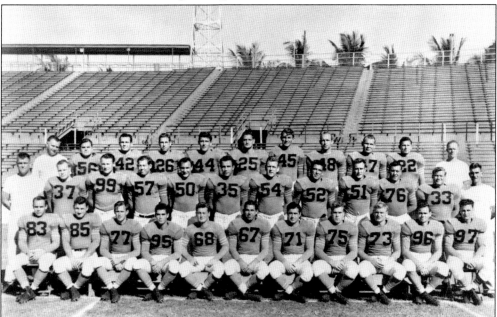

In 1948, Harvey Hester formed and funded the ill-fated Miami Seahawks, a member of the All-American Conference. Every home game was met with torrential rainstorms, and the lack of attendance was devastating. Hester's venture foundered and collapsed after one season. Professional football did not return until Joe Robbie started the Dolphins in the mid-1960s. Although the names of the players have been lost to the mists of time, this is one of the few team photographs of the Seahawks known to exist.

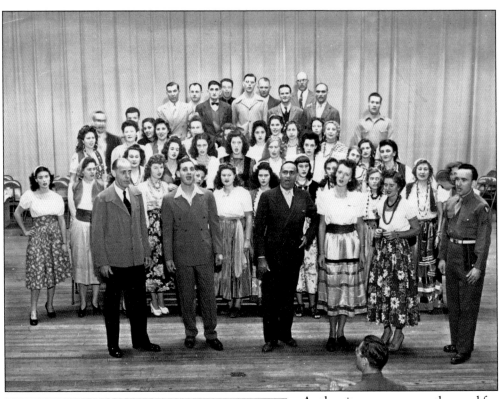

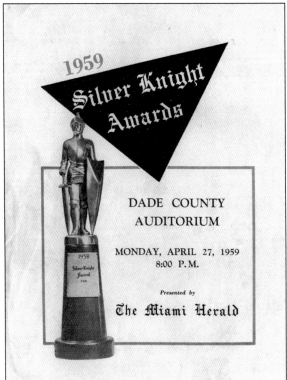

1959 Silver Knight Awards

DADE COUNTY
AUDITORIUM

MONDAY, APRIL 27, 1959
8:00 P.M.

Presented by

The Miami Herald

As the city grew, so grew the need for more cultural events and activities. The Miami Opera Guild, now the Greater Miami Opera Guild, began to offer regular winter-season opera performances, and today tickets are hot commodities. The guild is usually sold out for the season.

Since the late 1950s, the *Miami Herald* has sponsored the Silver Knight Awards (for many years, John and James Knight owned the *Herald*), which are given to high school students who are the highest achievers in their fields in many categories and disciplines. The cover of the 1959 awards ceremony is shown here.

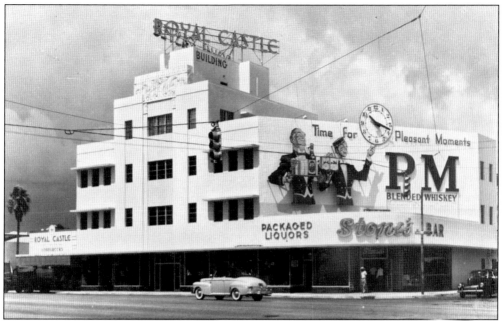

No story of Miami can be complete without noting how much everybody loved Royal Castle! From the 15¢ hamburgers to the big mugs of birch beer and the honeybuns, from the eggs freshly made with a big piece of butter to the great hot coffee, it was everybody's favorite. With a change of ownership, the chain faded to one lone restaurant at Northwest Twenty-seventh Avenue and Seventy-ninth Street. Prior to new ownership moving the offices and commissary to Northwest Sixty-second Street, the chain was headquartered at Tenth Street and Biscayne Boulevard. The restaurant was ensconced at the southeast corner of the building.

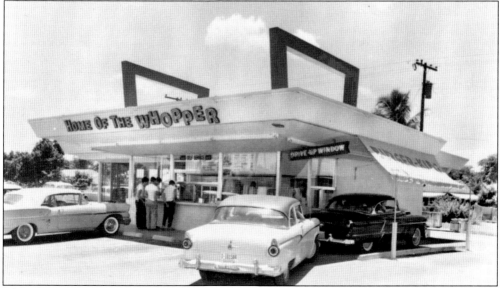

There is no question that another chain, also founded in Miami, had a hand in "RC's" undoing, and one of the very first stores of the now second-largest national chain of restaurants—Burger King—is shown in Miami. By the years of the cars, it appears that this photograph was taken around 1956.

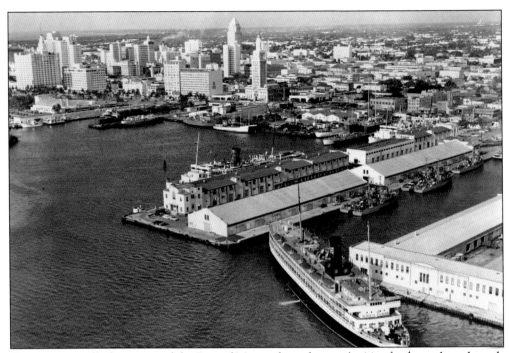

Two exceptionally fine views of the Port of Miami show the city looking both south and north from the port. In the top view, the Miami News Building (later the Freedom Tower), the various Biscayne Boulevard hotels, the Bayfront Park Auditorium, the Dade County Courthouse, and the high-rises of downtown are visible. In the lower view, looking north, the piers are clearly shown with the Belcher Oil tanks behind them. The tall building is the Lindsey Hopkins Hotel, for some years home of Tech High School and later the headquarters of the Dade County School Board.

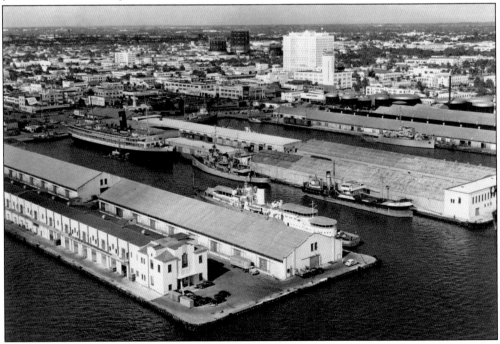

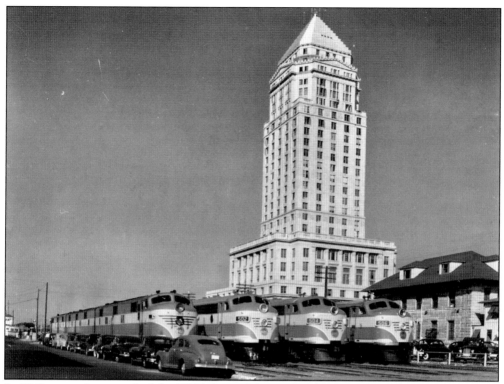

In 1947, upon the arrival of the FEC's beautiful new diesel locomotives, photographer Harry Wolfe posed four sets of them in the magnificent red-and-yellow paint scheme on the south side of the courthouse, giving the appearance, as the FEC was wont to do, that the courthouse was the Miami station.

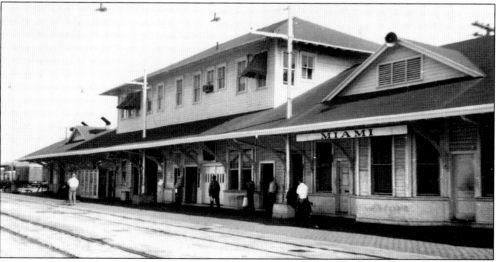

The FEC's Miami passenger station is pictured in all its glory. Opened in late 1912 at what would become, with the 1921 street numbering change, 200 Northwest First Avenue, this wonderful depot was the place where millions of people first set foot on terra firma within the city of Miami. Torn down between September and November 1963, the station remains a fond memory for innumerable train travelers.

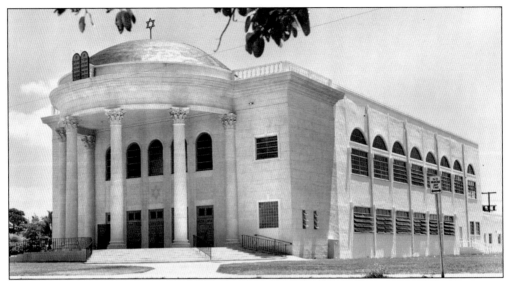

Houses of worship were and are an important part of Miami's history. Temple Beth Jacob, now on Coral Way, was founded downtown by Isadore Cohen in the early years of the 20th century. Its new sanctuary is shown here. Although the neighborhood has changed dramatically, the temple continues to draw members of the Jewish faith from all parts of Greater Miami.

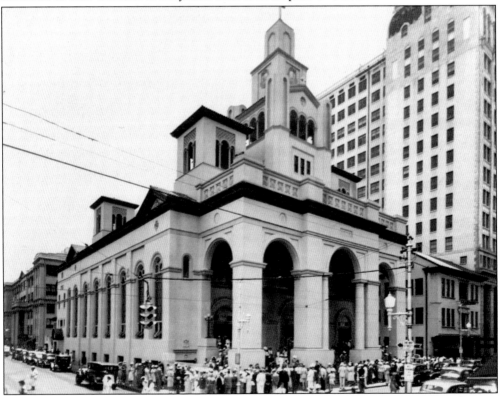

Gesu Catholic Church and School are, similarly to Temple Beth Jacob, pioneers in Miami history. The church has a long tradition of ministering to the Catholic residents of Miami. Still very active, it has been part of downtown Miami for close to 100 years.

Ralph Renick was Miami's most beloved, respected, and trusted broadcast journalist. He convinced Col. Mitchell Wolfson to let him start television broadcasting in Florida, and they chose the call letters "WTVJ" when the station went on the air in 1948. Ralph Renick stands under the marquee of the former Wometco movie theater around 1952; the theater was converted to the television station where he remained for almost 30 years. His "Good night and may the good news be yours" closing became a South Florida catchphrase.

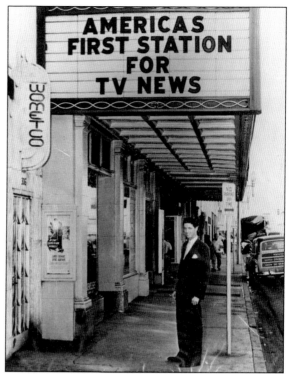

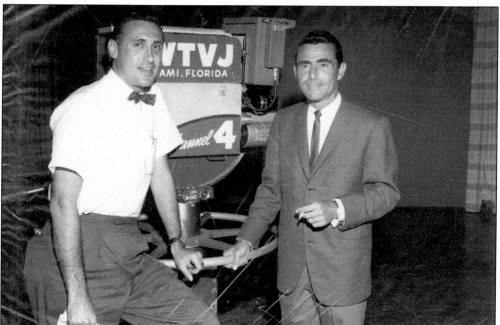

Because of Renick, Channel 4 in Miami gained national renown as the first local station in America to broadcast news and the first to air a television editorial, just two of a long line of honors. One did not, no matter how big or powerful, turn down an invitation to appear with Renick. Here longtime WTVJ producer Bud Weil, at left, chats with Rod Serling of *Twilight Zone* fame prior to Serling's interview with Renick.

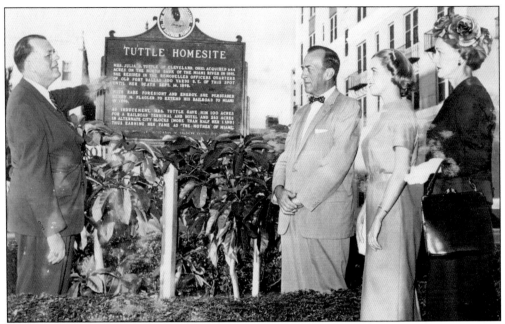

On December 5, 1959, the Historical Association of Southern Florida dedicated one of its major cast monuments to memorializing Julia Tuttle's homesite. Harry Tuttle is at left and Julia Tuttle Usher is second from right; the other two are unidentified. With Miami's unending rebuilding, the entire plaque vanished. It supposedly turned up in a Tallahassee warehouse, following which it again disappeared and has never been seen since.

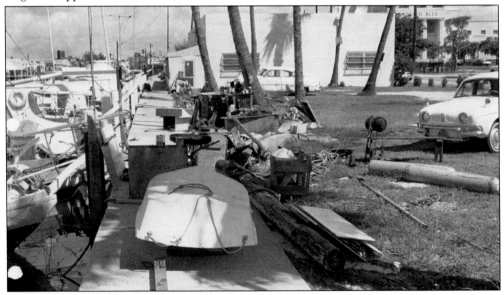

For many years, the Miami Pioneers were a major and important influence on Miami's history. As time passed and the requirement that in order to be a member one must have arrived in Miami by 1925 or be legacy of someone who had, membership dwindled until the difficult decision to amalgamate with another historic organization was made. The building shown here is the clubhouse of the Pioneers, now long gone following their move to the Miami Woman's Club Building on North Bayshore Drive prior to the merger with the Natives of Dade.

"The times they were a'-changin'," and with those changes came the end of numerous Miami buildings and attractions, lost due to changing tastes and the need to build new retail developments and housing. The Columbus Hotel on Biscayne Boulevard, once a mainstay of downtown and a rendezvous of business people and travelers and for many years the city ticket office location for Eastern Air Lines, is no longer as huge high-rises are being erected along Biscayne Boulevard.

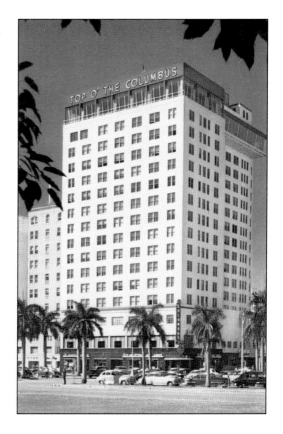

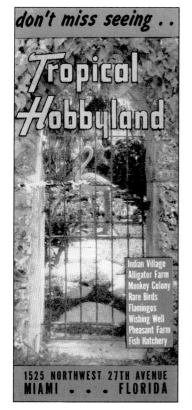

Tourist attractions also fell on hard economic times as people lost interest in seeing alligator wrestling, caged monkeys, flamingos, and macaws. Tropical Hobbyland, one of Miami's most popular attractions for many years at 1525 Northwest Twenty-seventh Avenue, could not withstand the onslaught of a mushrooming populace and the need for—in the developer's minds—better space usage.

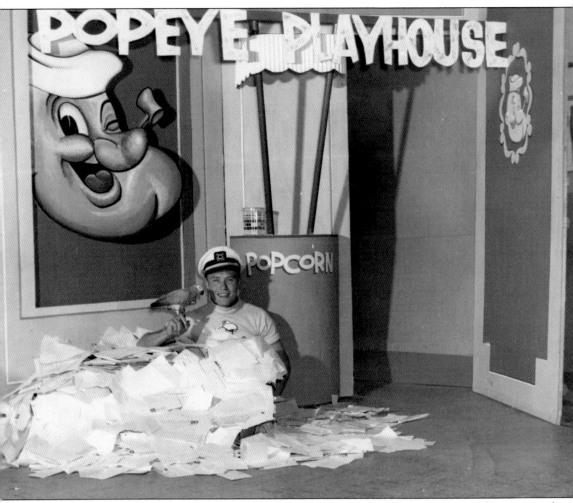

"Skipper Chuck" Zink was—as can be seen by the flood of mail almost covering him—one of Miami's most beloved local personalities. Genuine, gracious, cordial, and a true gentleman, he hosted Miami's longest continuously running children's program on WTVJ. He finished his career as a local radio talk and music show host, and his death in early 2006 was met with shock and disbelief, his funeral so large that mourners stood outside to remember a man who had been part of Miami's history from the mid-1950s.

Seven

A WORLD-CLASS CITY MOVES TOWARD THE FUTURE

No other city in the country has sustained what Miami has. From its days as a tourism mecca, through the boom and bust, renewed by the servicemen stationed here in World War II, getting through the relatively calm 1950s, welcoming and providing homes, jobs, and business opportunities for an immense flood of refugees from Castro's communism, to an enormous burst of skyscraper building since the mid-1980s, Miami remains one of the most fascinating, unique, and puzzling cities in America.

When the name "Miami" is mentioned in the national news media, few think of just the city of Miami. Miami has come to mean the entire county (renamed Miami-Dade several years ago), and though covering only a fraction of the county's 2,000-plus square miles, Miami, the city, is the county seat and the government center. It is the home of great hospitals, including Bascom Palmer Eye Institute at Jackson Memorial Hospital, the number-one eye-care facility in America according to *US News and World Report*; a nationally recognized trauma center; one of the nation's busiest airports; the busiest cruise port in the world; and a college within the city's limits—Miami-Dade—that was, for most of the years it was a community college, considered the finest community college in the nation.

There were problems, from poverty, to crime, to being rated as having the third or fourth most congested highways in the country, to being the focal point for almost all refugees from Central and South America and the Caribbean. Miami continues to endure its share, but no matter how great the difficulty, the city continues to roll with the punches, pick itself up off the ground, and begin fresh and new.

So it has been since Julia Tuttle convinced Henry Flagler to extend the railroad to the shores of Biscayne Bay; since the devastation of the 1926 hurricane; since the land boom went bust and with the Depression following; since World War II and the Cuban immigration; and so will it always continue to be.

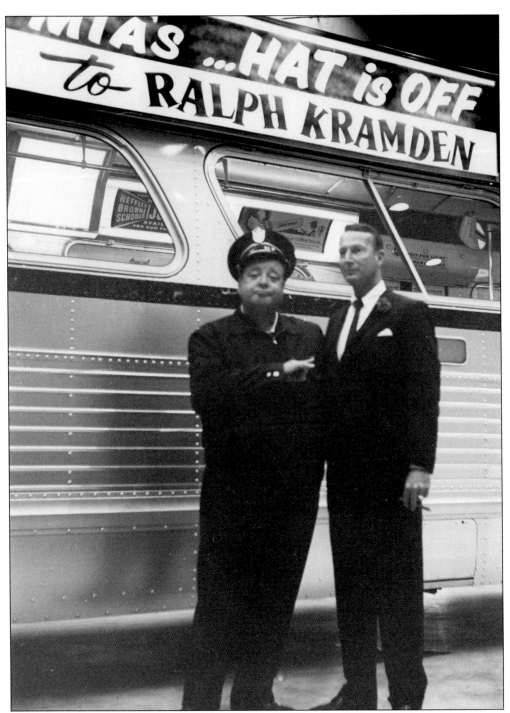

Jackie Gleason was loved almost beyond words, and when he moved his television show to Miami Beach in the 1970s, it began the beach's revitalization. Because he played Ralph Kramden, the New York bus driver, Miami's Metropolitan Transit Authority honored the Great One with a plaque and a series of displays featuring Jackie, shown here, and his bus-driving alter ego. It is not known who the man on the right is.

Beauty is in the eye of the beholder, and whether it is the Miami sunset, a view of Biscayne Bay, the flora, people, or police equines, there is an almost unlimited amount of beauty in the Magic City. One of Miami's great beauties of the female persuasion was a schoolteacher for many years at, among other Miami schools, Arcola Lake, Horace Mann, and West Little River. Gentle, elegant, and beloved by family and friends, Myrna Bramson poses poolside in the Miami sunshine.

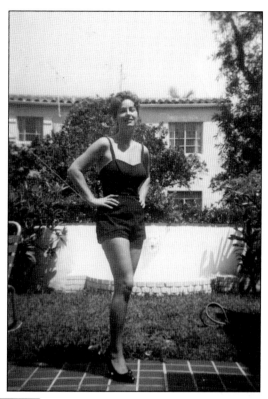

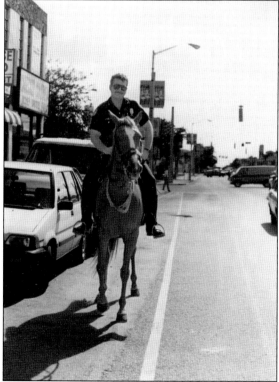

Just north of Seventy-ninth Street on Biscayne Boulevard, police officer Dave Hill is up on his beautiful mount, patrolling the area around the Seventy-ninth Street Shopping Center. Miami's police mounted unit is the department's greatest single asset, the gentleness and beauty of the horses matched only by the genuine cordiality and friendliness of their riders. Officer Hill is a perfect example.

121

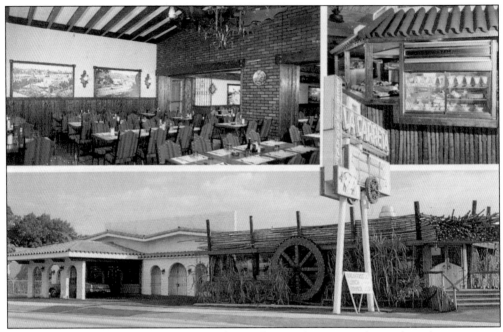

Fortunately for Miamians, the coming of Cubans following the Castro takeover brought new cuisine and restaurants that now serve black, white, and Hispanic Miami residents, their friends, and guests with wonderful food, interesting drinks, and, above all, the always-welcome café Cubano, an enjoyable end to any meal at La Carreta on Southwest Eighth Street in Little Havana.

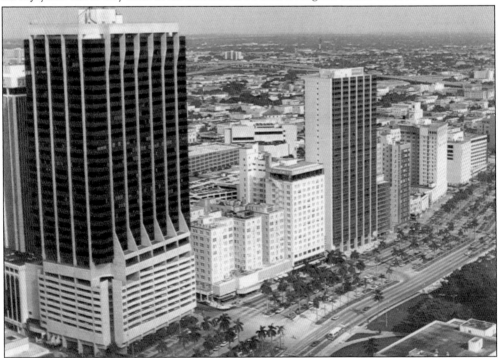

In the process of being completely remade, a new Miami reaches skyward, replacing buildings—in this case, downtown on Biscayne Boulevard—built, for the most part, in the 1920s and 1930s.

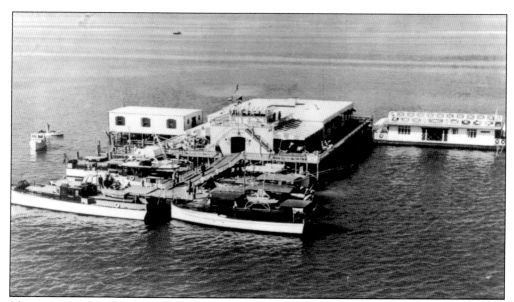

The water is and will always be a major asset to Miami. Whether the drivers using the various causeways, the kids playing in the surf, the people fishing in the numerous rivers and canals, or the fortunate few who maintain weekend abodes at Stiltsville, literally out in the Atlantic, Miami's water and waterways are a central part of their lives.

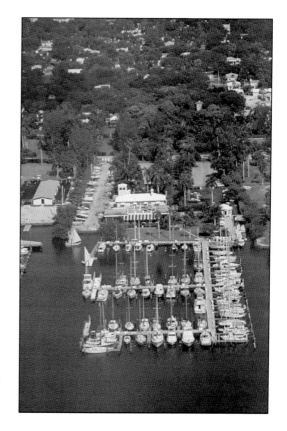

Miami's weather and proximity to so many navigable waterways, including the Atlantic Intracoastal Waterway, make boat ownership an added plus. The various shapes and sizes of sail- and motor-powered boats make for an interesting design in this superb aerial of Coral Reef Yacht Club on South Bayshore Drive in Coconut Grove.

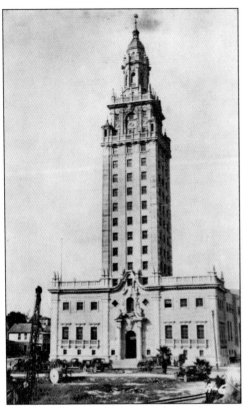

The Miami News Building/Freedom Tower was built on hallowed ground, the site of the first FEC Railway station in Miami. Any plans for it becoming a museum should include the site's history and not be limited solely to the Cuban experience, which certainly deserves remembrance but should not exclude the past prior to 1960. These two views show the building in all its stateliness, first still under construction in 1924–1925 and, on May 20, 1975, as the beacon of hope and freedom to newly arriving Cuban immigrants. Having survived innumerable plans, the future of the building, other than being saved from demolition, is still hazy at best and unknown at worst.

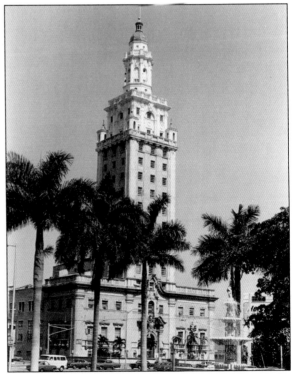

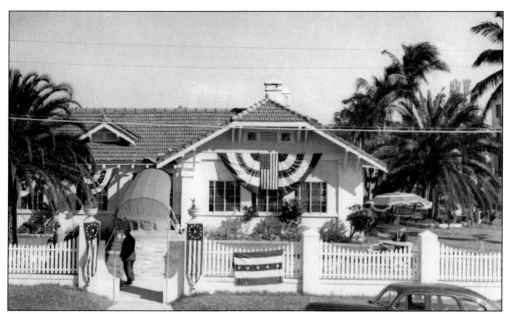

Among the great philanthropic success stories in the history of Miami is that of the Miami Jewish Home and Hospital at Douglas Gardens, Northeast Second Avenue at Fifty-second Street. Originally opened in 1945 on Southwest Twelfth Avenue in the Riverside section, the first building, shown here, housed just 23 elderly Jewish widows and widowers.

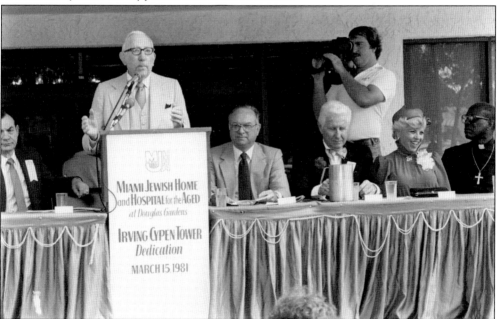

Thirty-six years later, the community witnessed the dedication of the Irving Cypen Tower, named for the man who has been the driving force behind the incredible growth of this major health-care center, the only four-star rehabilitation center in South Florida. Shown at the dedication are, from left to right, Harold Beck, Congressman Claude Pepper, Sydney Aronovitz, Judge Irving Cypen, Hazel Cypen, and Rev. Theodore Gibson. (Courtesy Miami Jewish Home and Hospital at Douglas Gardens.)

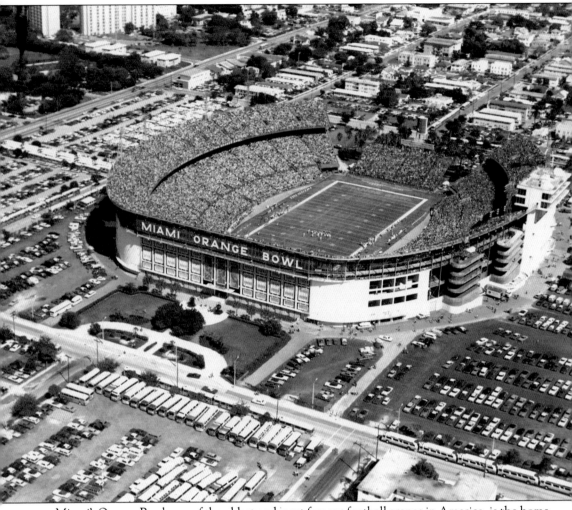

Miami's Orange Bowl, one of the oldest and most famous football arenas in America, is the home field of the University of Miami Hurricanes and Miami High School. Built on what was originally a baseball field, the site became Roddy Burdine Stadium prior to being named the Orange Bowl. Currently plans are underway for a complete renovation of the city-owned facility.

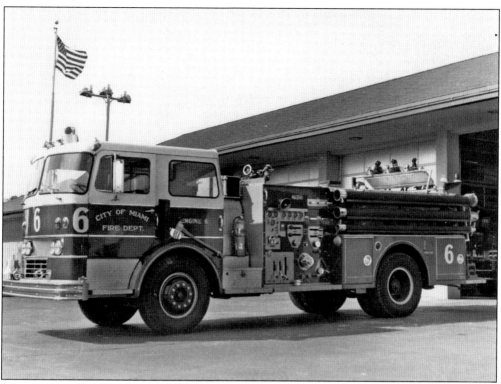

Miami's Class One Fire Department is one of the most decorated and recognized fire-rescue organizations in America, called upon to assist wherever disaster strikes nationwide. Miami's crews were involved in the rescue and recovery efforts following the Oklahoma City bombing, the 9/11 tragedy, and Hurricane Wilma, as well as many other events both locally and out of state. Here Engine No. 6 sits for its portrait in February 1977.

For the joint FEC Railway–City of Miami Centennial in 1996, many organizations throughout the city contributed by donating funds or organizing events. Among the participants, LaSalle High School on South Miami Avenue, adjacent to Mercy Hospital, presented a salute honoring the pioneer families, both black and white, of Coconut Grove. Held on April 26, the event included a special display of Coconut Grove and Miami memorabilia supplied from the collection of the author.

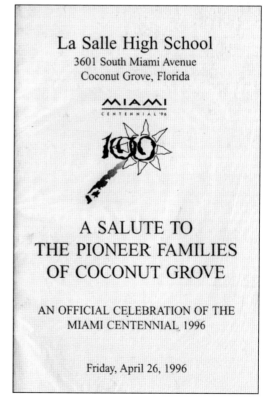

La Salle High School
3601 South Miami Avenue
Coconut Grove, Florida

MIAMI
CENTENNIAL '96

100

A SALUTE TO
THE PIONEER FAMILIES
OF COCONUT GROVE

AN OFFICIAL CELEBRATION OF THE
MIAMI CENTENNIAL 1996

Friday, April 26, 1996

Discover Thousands of Local History Books
Featuring Millions of Vintage Images

Arcadia Publishing, the leading local history publisher in the United States, is committed to making history accessible and meaningful through publishing books that celebrate and preserve the heritage of America's people and places.

Find more books like this at
www.arcadiapublishing.com

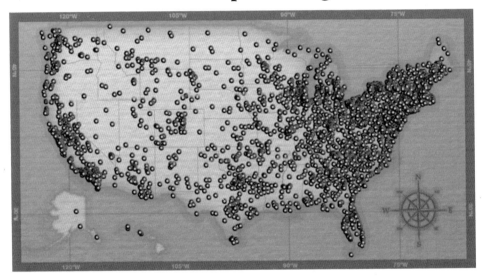

Search for your hometown history, your old stomping grounds, and even your favorite sports team.

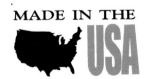